WRITING THEIR BODIES

WRITING THEIR BODIES

Restoring Rhetorical Relations at the Carlisle Indian School

SARAH KLOTZ

UTAH STATE UNIVERSITY PRESS
Logan

Published by Utah State University Press
An imprint of University Press of Colorado
245 Century Circle, Suite 202
Louisville, Colorado 80027

The University Press of Colorado is a proud member of the Association of University Presses.

The University Press of Colorado is a cooperative publishing enterprise supported, in part, by Adams State University, Colorado State University, Fort Lewis College, Metropolitan State University of Denver, Regis University, University of Colorado, University of Northern Colorado, University of Wyoming, Utah State University, and Western Colorado University.

∞ This paper meets the requirements of the ANSI/NISO Z39.48–1992 (Permanence of Paper).

ISBN: 978-1-64642-086-5 (paperback)
ISBN: 978-1-64642-087-2 (ebook)
https://doi.org/10.7330/9781646420872

Library of Congress Cataloging-in-Publication Data

Names: Klotz, Sarah, author.
Title: Writing their bodies : restoring rhetorical relations at the Carlisle Indian School / by Sarah Klotz.
Description: Logan : Utah State University Press, 2021. | Includes bibliographical references and index. | Summary: "1879–1918, the Carlisle Indian Industrial School, the first off-reservation Indigenous American boarding school, housed 10,000 students and was a prototype for boarding schools across the continent. Analyzes pedagogical philosophies and curricular materials through the perspective of written and visual student texts during the first three-year term"—Provided by publisher.
Identifiers: LCCN 2020051116 (print) | LCCN 2020051117 (ebook) | ISBN 9781646420865 (paperback) | ISBN 9781646420872 (ebook)
Subjects: LCSH: United States Indian School (Carlisle, Pa.) | Off-reservation boarding schools—Pennsylvania—Carlisle—History. | Picture-writing. | English language—Study and teaching—Pennsylvania—Carlisle—History. | Indians of North America—Cultural assimilation—United States. | Indians of North America—Pennsylvania—Carlisle—Ethnic identity—History. | Indians of North America—Pennsylvania—Carlisle—Social conditions—History. | Indians of North America—Education—Pennsylvania—Carlisle—History. | Racism in education—Pennsylvania—Carlisle—History.
Classification: LCC E97.6.C2 K56 2021 (print) | LCC E97.6.C2 (ebook) | DDC 974.8/01—dc23
LC record available at https://lccn.loc.gov/2020051116
LC ebook record available at https://lccn.loc.gov/2020051117

Cover illustration: "Telling Something," © Candy Nartonis

For my mother, who made everything possible.

CONTENTS

PREFACE

In October 1879, Colonel Richard Henry Pratt began his experiment in Indian education at the Carlisle Indian Industrial School. Prior to opening the school, Pratt had fought in the Civil War, commanded a unit of Buffalo Soldiers in Oklahoma, and served in a cavalry regiment during campaigns against Indigenous nations of the Southern Plains. Pratt's military background makes clear the settler-colonial violence behind the off-reservation school even as his rhetoric promised a new era of progress for the American Indian. Pratt developed his strategy of Indian education at Fort Marion in Florida between 1875 and 1878, when the War Department appointed him warden of seventy-two prisoners of the allied Kiowa, Comanche, Cheyenne, and Arapahoe tribes. Based upon his success "civilizing" the prisoners and hoping that Pratt had finally provided a solution to the Indian Problem, the federal government gave him the abandoned Army barracks in Carlisle, Pennsylvania, to open the first off-reservation boarding school.

Between 1879 and its closing in 1918, Carlisle would house over 10,000 students and serve as a prototype for boarding schools on and off reservations across the continent. While we now view the school through the lens of its hulking ambition and generational impacts, Carlisle opened with very few students—eighty-two children, both boys and girls from the Lakota Rosebud and Pine Ridge agencies in South Dakota and some relatives and recruits of Fort Marion prisoners. The War Department demanded that Pratt focus his recruiting efforts on Lakota youths to dismantle resistance to the US government only three years after Custer's defeat at the Battle of the Greasy Grass (Little Big Horn), reasoning that Western tribes would be deterred from acting against the US government if their children were hostages thousands of miles to the east.[1] Parents agreed to a three-year term for their children to attend school. This study focuses on these first students because their rhetorical tactics formed in an environment of early intercultural contact. The school's curriculum and philosophy were not yet fully formed, which made space for students to incorporate their existing literacies into their educational environment.

DOI: 10.7330/9781646420872.c000a

They found opportunities to rebel and to refigure the scope of rhetorical possibility at school. Ultimately, I argue that these early students developed communicative tactics at school that aimed to bring about their visions of Indigenous futurity once they returned to their homelands.

Carlisle became the educational arm of a body of US government policies that culminated in the 1887 Dawes Act. We now recognize this period as the Assimilation Era. As Siobhan Senier summarizes, the Dawes Bill "proposed to divide up communally held tribal lands 'in severalty,' allotting a Jeffersonian 160 acres to each head of family. The Indian land would be held in trust for twenty-five years, at the end of which time American Indians would be made U.S. citizens and given individual titles to that land" (Senier 2001, 5). While supporters touted the legislation as a means to finally extend full citizenship to Native peoples, the most lasting effect of the bill was to open massive tracts of land to white settlement. Ultimately Native Americans lost 90 million acres, or two-thirds, of their landholdings (Senier 2001, 5). As historian Frederick Hoxie argues, assimilationist policies proceeded in two phases. The first operated on the belief that Native Americans could earn citizenship by proving their civilization—that is, by adopting the language, culture, and individual land ownership of settler society. This study focuses on students reacting to the educational policy conditions of this first stage. The second phase involved a continued effort to incorporate Native Americans into Euro-American society without the promise of full citizenship and equality (Hoxie 1984, xxi). At Carlisle, the second phase brought about a shift in pedagogical priorities, from a complete curriculum in trades, language, and arts and sciences to a strictly vocational program so that Indian students could become laborers and servants for Euro-Americans. This study focuses on Carlisle's first years because they show an assimilationist worldview in process, with gaps in logic and implementation and a significant degree of intercultural negotiation around what the future would look like for Native peoples in North America.

A number of scholars have turned their attention to the off-reservation boarding school, examining both the particularities of individual institutions (Child 1998; Landrum 2019; Lomawaima 1994) and the philosophy, policies, and social impact of the movement writ large (Adams 1995; Archuleta, Child, and Lomawaima 2000; Fear-Segal 2007; Gram 2015; Katanski 2005; Lomawaima and McCarty 2006). Interest in the off-reservation boarding school has stretched across disciplines from history to American studies, literature, Native American / Indigenous studies, education, and linguistics. In each case, Carlisle features prominently as the earliest attempt at what would become a national trend.

Each of these scholars has contributed to how we understand the day-to-day experiences of students and how they negotiated the schooling process through "creativity, adaptability, and resistance to the federal agenda of transformation" (Lomawaima 1994, xi). My study is unique in its narrowly focused time frame and scope. Rather than examining the forty-year tenure of Carlisle, I focus on the years 1875–1885 and the very first students at Fort Marion, Hampton, and then Carlisle to enter into the government assimilationist project through education. This narrow scope allows me to read the archive closely for rhetorical practices that students engaged, revised, and developed to face a new era of colonization. By centering my attention on the earliest students, I follow the thread from colonial violence in the Indian Wars on the Southern Plains to colonial violence in the boarding school. Most importantly, the scope of this study allows us to understand assimilationist education as an inconsistent, developing, and negotiated process where Indigenous rhetors—prisoners, students, and leaders—impacted the curriculum, norms, and practices of the institutions in which they were confined.

The boarding school movement is one of many historic and ongoing attempts by the United States to achieve what Audra Simpson calls its "monocultural aspirations" (2014, 22). As such, boarding schools attempt to extinguish markers of ethnic and national difference such as clothing, hair, labor practices, and, most significantly, language. As Fear-Segal and Rose argue,

> the purpose of the education campaign matched previous policies: dispossessing Native peoples of their lands and extinguishing their existence as distinct groups that threatened the nation-building project of the United States. These objectives were effectively masked from the white public by a long-established American educational rhetoric that linked schooling to both democracy and individual advancement. (Fear-Segal and Rose 2016, 2)

Through benevolent rhetoric, the nationalistic aims of the boarding school came to be seen as not only the best thing for the United States but also the best thing for thousands of Indigenous young people who were legally required to attend boarding school after the passing of the compulsory attendance law in 1891. In the early years, however, attendance was not compulsory, and Pratt had to rely on diplomacy and coercion to recruit students. Students' early resistant rhetorics at school—such as hunger striking or running away—impacted how Pratt's project was received by their nations at home. Every time a student became sick or died or when parents visited and found their children being mistreated, it became more difficult for Pratt to recruit and retain students. In this sense, student resistance was particularly powerful during their first term, and the strategies they developed would continue to reemerge in fights for territorial and intellectual sovereignty for decades to come.

As often as scholars have studied the resistant strategies of students, they have also noted the ways that boarding schools became spaces for the development of pan-Indian or intertribal identities.[2] Robert Warrior identifies Fort Marion as the site where the earliest form of intertribal sociality developed as prisoners shared songs and developed "the ethic of respect for particularity and sameness that remains an ideal of inter-tribal gatherings and organizations" (Warrior 2005, 107). Brenda Child points us to the "Star of Bethlehem" quilt design that girls learned at Carlisle, which has since been incorporated into tribal life of the Upper Midwest, where star quilts are now the most highly prized item at give-aways during tribal ceremonies. She writes, "[L]ike the star blanket the boarding school has become part of our pan-Indian identity" (Child 1998, 4). The concept of a rhetoric of relations advanced in the following pages contributes to how we understand the boarding school as a site of intertribal coalition development. By demonstrating how expressive tra-ditions such as Plains Sign Talk and pictography—technologies already used for intertribal communication on the Southern Plains—became shared rhetorics among youths from different nations at Carlisle, I argue that these rhetorical relations pushed back against the pressure for students to learn only English as a shared tongue. Also significant are the ways that resistance became a common ground where students from different nations built loyalty to one another through their shared opposition to school authorities (Lomawaima 1994, xiii). When I discuss Ernest White Thunder conceiving of his fellow students as the audience for his hunger strike or Harriet Mary Elder writing about how her fellow students behave better than the Euro-American children she meets at Sunday School, we can see how students banded together to maintain their Indigenous identities at an institution designed to reroute their energies toward settler cultural practices.

Even as this study focuses on the innovative rhetorics that Carlisle students and Fort Marion prisoners used to ensure tribal survivance, it is equally important to understand the violent constraints within which these rhetors acted. As Brenda Child has argued, "punishments for speaking tribal languages included beatings, swats from rulers, having one's mouth washed out with soap or lye, or being locked in the school jail" (Child 1998, 28). At Carlisle, "punishments ranged from being locked in the guardhouse for a week at a time to dietary restrictions, to occasional beatings" (Katanski 2005, 56). At Fort Marion and Carlisle, punishments were handed down by peers in military-style tribunals to displace the responsibility for the cruelty from Pratt and other school authorities and further break down the students' solidarity with one another. As Risling Baldy has pointed out as well, "survivors of the boarding school experience report that they were victims of rampant physical and sexual abuse often perpetrated by boarding school officials, teachers, and government agents" (Risling Baldy 2018, 15). Many of the embodied and material rhetorics that I discuss in the following pages cannot be understood outside the context of the corporeal forms of abuse and coercion that occurred and continue to have generational impacts in Indigenous communities. Each of these elements of the boarding school experience—resistance, violence, intertribal coalitional development, homesickness, and running away—illuminate the conditions and constraints under which the earliest students lived and told their stories.

This book has two primary aspirations. The first is to bring the embodied and material rhetorics of Carlisle students—what I term the *rhetoric of relations*—into the ongoing scholarly conversation on Indigenous expressive traditions. My archival methodology is indebted to decades of scholarship that places Native American alphabetic literary and autobiographical texts in relation to other textual and extratextual practices ranging from wampum belts to pictographic writing to the Cherokee syllabary to Plains hide painting to basket weaving and beyond. Lisa Brooks (2008), Matt Cohen (2010), Ellen Cushman (2011), Stephanie Fitzgerald (2008), and Philip Round (2010), to name just a few key figures, have demonstrated how performance and orality interact with textual and material productions to make meaning in Native American / Indigenous rhetoric. My task, as I see it, is to demonstrate how the material and embodied facets of Native American communication became tools for survivance in the particular forms that captivity took in the Assimilation Era—imprisonment at Fort Marion and other US military sites, sequestration in off-reservation boarding schools, and "outing" on Pennsylvania farms. This study shows how—in the surveilled, carceral environment—embodied and material practices allowed Indigenous rhetors to engage in covert and strategic continuance of their cultural identities. Ultimately, I argue these relational rhetorical modes allowed Indigenous prisoners and students, as well as their audiences, to imagine a future for Indigenous nations beyond the immediate conditions of violence and erasure during the Assimilation Era.

The second ambition of this book is to illuminate the fantasy of benevolence that propelled settler colonization during this period. I aim to dispel such fantasies in our contemporary rhetorical landscape as well. Education has been and continues to be a site where the benevolent impulse allows language and literacy educators to standardize, limit, and erase their students' means of expression. This is a nationalistic and assimilationist practice that serves the interests of the settler state, not the students we claim to empower through education. This book seeks to illuminate the extraordinary expressive repositories that Indigenous rhetors draw upon to survive, persist, and build futures from within the institutions that perpetrate violence against them. This study looks to and beyond the written word—to pictographic writing, hunger striking, sign language, periodical publication, suicide, and more—to trace the full scope of rhetorical modes that Indigenous prisoners and students engaged within their respective captivities. This study traces processes of assimilation and resistance to dispel the fantasy of benevolence and replace it with an account of settler violence and Indigenous survivance in the Assimilation Era.

A NOTE ON NAMING AND TERMINOLOGY

To clarify some of the choices I have made, as well as the areas where ambiguity in naming can illuminate the experiences of Carlisle students, it is useful to enumerate the approach I have taken to the names of students and their nations. Whenever possible, I refer to the peoples making up the First Nations of North America as either *Indigenous, American Indian,* or *Native American.* I use the terms interchangeably in an attempt to be inclusive of the largest scope of intellectual traditions in the fields of Native American / Indigenous studies. Documents often refer to Native nations by misnomers or imprecise language, such as *Sioux,* and I will regularly reframe those misnamings when I am not using direct quotes and refer to Native peoples by the names they call themselves. Any mistakes I have made are entirely my own fault and no reflection of the work of my generous teachers.

I use the term *Indian* to represent a figuration of settler society. The term *Indian* appears often in the writings of Richard Henry Pratt, for example, and when referring to his writing, I use the term to underline his racialist and colonial views. The term *Indian* also allows me to talk about the rhetorical construction of Indigenous peoples deployed by settlers, and I often use the term to indicate how settler society creates shifting images of Indigenous peoples to justify their ongoing, unjust occupation of the American continent.

The names of students present another set of challenges. To create clarity and consistency across various archival documents and ensure that readers can easily find these students' texts in digital repositories such as the Carlisle Indian School Digital Resource Center, I refer to students most often by the names they had at school. I will indicate parenthetically, whenever possible, their names before coming to school. Students' names were changed almost immediately upon entering Carlisle. In some cases, such as Ernest White Thunder, the student received their father's name as a surname to codify a patrilineal line of descent. In other cases, students were called by names that have no connection to their kinship relations or the names they are called in their communities. Rutherford B. Hayes is an example of this pattern. Finally, some students are anonymized in the periodical record such as the "Nez Perce girl" discussed in chapter 4. I have attempted to match these anonymous students to records that give Anglicized versions of their names, in this case Harriet Mary, then Harriet Mary Elder, then Harriet Mary Stuart. Close attention to how these students' names changed over time will give the reader insight into the ways that Carlisle authorities demonstrated their power to name and order things in the world. While using multiple names or naming students or their nations in ways that differ from the documentary record, I may be introducing a level of ambiguity to the stories that follow. It is my hope that readers can transform this ambiguity into awareness about how the power to name is a fundamental aspect of self-determination. Carlisle's documentary record attempts to erase Native names, and this study uses naming as a reparative act.

ACKNOWLEDGMENTS

I have been writing this book in many places and for many years. This book has been written on the territory of the Mechoopda Maidu, the Tongva, the Anishinaabeg, and the Nipmuc. I acknowledge these nations for their stewardship of the land where I have been privileged to write, think, and teach. I also acknowledge the Indigenous young people that I write about in this project: Etahdleuh Doanmoe, Ernest White Thunder, Charles Kihega, Harriet Mary Elder, and so many more. Their courage and ingenuity are part of a story that must be told and retold. I hope I have captured their messages with sincerity and respect.

A project like this only happens through the dedicated labors of many. I have benefited beyond measure from many teachers, mentors, friends, and colleagues. I am grateful to Malea Powell, who took on a mentee living 3,000 miles away because she saw promise in my work. Malea provided intellectual, emotional, and professional support when I was sure this project would never come to fruition. Without her, I doubt you would be reading this book today. Malea is an exemplary scholar who also happens to be an exemplary human being. It continues to be my privilege to learn from her. Thank you also to my first mentor, Jenny Putzi, who taught me how to read texts and make sense of archives when I was an undergraduate. She convinced me that I could be a scholar. I did not come from a background where becoming a professor was a possibility; Jenny made it so. Her support and kindness keep me going on this long and winding academic road. Thanks to Mark Jerng and Carl Whithaus, who gave me the space to write a dissertation at the fraught nexus of literary and rhetorical studies, while helping me to become a better writer in the process. Thanks to Alan Taylor, Kelly Wisecup, Angela Calcaterra, Ari Kelman, Emily Legg, and Stephanie Fitzgerald, whose scholarship and camaraderie have helped me to become a better thinker. Thanks to so many friends who have read drafts and listened to me talk about the project: Meg Sparling, Cheryl Ching, Bethany

Hopkins, Dyani Johns Taff, Hannah Burdette, Leslie Henson, and Heather Springer, just to name a few.

Because this book draws so substantially on archival documents, I am particularly indebted to the archivists and librarians at the Cumberland County Historical Society, the Beinecke Rare Book and Manuscript Library, and the Dickinson College Archives and Special Collections. The work of Jim Gerencser, Kate Theimer, and Richard Tritt has been indispensable. Thank you for your intellectual companionship throughout this process.

Thank you to my small family, which has been beside me through all of the writing and thinking—my constant, quiet companions. My love, Jay. My dogs, Zooey and Emma. There is nothing more comforting than knowing you are right there, waiting for me to get off the computer and go for a walk in the sun.

Finally, I gratefully acknowledge the various funders who made the work possible. Thank you in particular to the NCTE/CCCC Emergent Researcher Award, which provided funds for me to travel to archives when as I worked in various teaching-oriented positions that did not provide research support. Thank you also to the American Antiquarian Society, for funding my travel to the 2013 summer seminar Indigenous Cultures of Print in Early America though the Isaiah Thomas Stipend. The seminar content and the scholars who I met there have created the foundation for much of my thinking in this book. Finally, thank you to the UC Humanities Research Institute for providing a dissertation year fellowship that allowed me to live and work in Carlisle as I was completing my first chapters on the Carlisle school.

WRITING THEIR BODIES

Introduction

TOWARD A RHETORIC OF RELATIONS

On June 25, 1880, photographer John N. Choate captured the slate of a Cheyenne student (re)named Rutherford B. Hayes. The top of the slate shows a series of words: apple, get, grew, all, trees. Below appears a short composition about a boy named Frank, in an apple tree, who plans to give an apple to Ann. Next is a letter composed to the student's father, informing him that "this here at Carlisle all the boys and girls like very nice school some boys and girls read in book every day work hard." At the bottom, a series of equations appears next to a pictographic rendering of a warrior riding a horse, labeled John Williams, the name of an Arapaho boy who started school the same day as R. B. Hayes[1] and was likely his classmate and friend. These inscriptions, erased for other lessons, have been preserved for 140 years in Choate's print.

The slate is a snapshot of the processes whereby the Carlisle Indian School attempted to assimilate Native children into cultural norms of whiteness. Everything from the student's assigned name to the composition about apples to the letter home indicates what, for Richard Henry Pratt (1973, 260) and his colleagues, could "kill the Indian, save the man."[2] Simultaneously, we glimpse another rhetorical tradition—a tradition that makes meaning within the communicative ecosystem of the Southern Plains, a tradition that is illegible to Carlisle's teachers. R. B. Hayes depicts a horse, a technology of war introduced by the Spanish in 1540 and long since an integral part of life for the Cheyenne, Comanche, Arapaho, and other Plains tribes. While the student learns alphabetic literacy, he produces pictographic literacy beside his newly acquired English words. He figures his Arapaho classmate as a warrior astride his horse, inscribing their shared story in both the English alphabet and Plains pictography. Just as his ancestors incorporated the horse into the fabric of tribal life, this student at school thousands of miles from home attempts to do the same with the English language.

This student's composition is not well-known. He did not become a famous essayist writing against settler colonialism in the late nineteenth

DOI: 10.7330/9781646420872.c000b

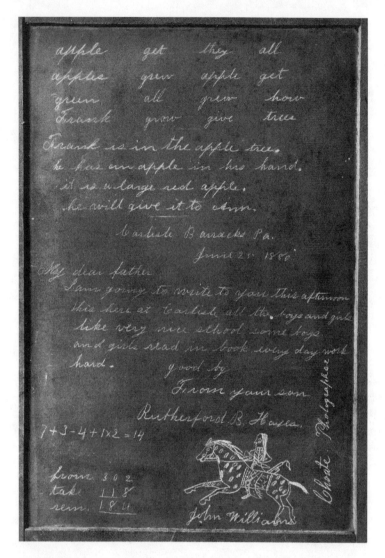

Figure 0.1. Indian School student's slate dated June 25, 1880. Photo by John N. Choate. Courtesy, Cumberland County Historical Society, Carlisle, PA.

century. He did not go on to publish a memoir of his time at boarding school. His ephemeral text is only preserved through the lens of a photographer who viewed it as a cultural curiosity. But if we want to understand how the history of composition has been intimately, even inextricably linked with colonization, then this student's work illuminates the complex processes whereby educators who believed completely in their own benevolence became instruments for the dispossession and de-culturation of Native peoples. In this book, I enumerate the dynamic routes of assimilation and resistance that characterized language and literacy training in the first years of the Carlisle school. My goal is not only to emphasize the colonialist history of American writing education but also to demonstrate how students developed multimodal, embodied rhetorics to resist and repurpose alphabetic literacy. I term these tactics *the rhetoric of relations.* As scholars engaged in the teaching of writing today, we cannot ignore the past and ongoing assimilationist motives of writing education. By grappling with this history, we can refuse to be well-intentioned yet complicit in ongoing processes of cultural erasure in our writing classrooms.

As I have pored over the texts produced during Carlisle's early years (photographs,[3] periodicals, letters, government reports, autobiographies), I have been struck by the impossibility of what I find—students like R. B. Hayes resisting and surviving the cultural genocide imposed on them. For one thing, these are young people still forming national identities—the first students ranged in age from seven years old to young adulthood. Their youth led the government to choose them for an acculturation experiment. For another, their texts are not only coerced but highly mediated. Students know that their teachers and the superintendent will read everything. They could be punished physically or humiliated in campus newspapers for making mistakes. In addition, these students are sick from new and strange food, an unfamiliar climate, and institutional epidemics such as tuberculosis, trachoma, measles, pneumonia, mumps, and influenza (Adams 1995, 125). To reckon with this rhetorical situation is to confront the impossible.

And yet, I am reminded of Gerald Vizenor's (1994, 41) story about watching a boy dancing at the Wahpeton Indian School in North Dakota, many years after Native children's first boarding school experiences at Carlisle:

> The observers participated in one of the most treacherous simulations of the tribal heart, a dance in chicken feathers to please the missionaries. Would we have been wiser to denounce the child at the time, to undermine the simulations of the dance in the presence of the superintendent? We should have told the child then and there our honest reaction to his dance, but we were his audience of solace. How could we be the assassins of his dreams of survivance?

Survivance is not elegant in this story. It is not pure or unadulterated tribal continuance. It is a process of performance, compromise, incorporation, humor, and discomfort. Survivance, a combination of survival and resistance, has become foundational to the study of Native rhetorics; yet in efforts to understand how rhetoric became a tool of survivance for Indigenous peoples of the late nineteenth century, we have too often focused on individuals whose texts appear in periodicals and books with a largely Euro-American readership. Zitkála-Šá, Charles Eastman, Sarah Winnemucca, and Luther Standing Bear achieved high levels of alphabetic literacy and gained access to the Euro-American print public sphere. My study locates rhetorics of survivance both in and beyond the written word because without a capacious and embodied rhetorical lens, early Carlisle students are impossible to recognize as "fully human subjects capable of tactical refigurings" (Powell 2002, 405). It is through embodied and material rhetorics that Richard Henry Pratt's first students pushed back against assimilationist education and maintained their cultural identities in the face of intractable odds.

I have termed these diverse and broad-ranging communicative tactics a "rhetoric of relations" in reference to the Lakota cultural symbol and ceremonial benediction Mitákuye Oyás'iŋ, or "all my relations." The orientation of human persons in ethical relation with non-human persons on a shared land base is echoed in the Kiowa maxim "behold, I stand in good relation to all things" and resonates with the cosmologies and lifeways of many Indigenous groups in the Americas (Lookingbill 2007, 31). "All my relations" encapsulates the belief that externally dissimilar beings share a common interiority; hence members of the Lakota Nation view themselves in relation to the Buffalo Nation and ascribe personhood and interiority to the stones, water, and plant life that share their homelands (Posthumus 2018, 15). Drawing on the writings of Vine Deloria, anthropologist David C. Posthumus (2018, 39) argues that American Indian beliefs and lifeways are "situated, temporal, experiential, and relational." This orientation is key to understanding Indigenous embodied and material rhetorics at Carlisle. I locate the rhetoric of relations in four distinct yet interrelated sites of interpretation and world making. First and foremost, this is a book about how relations among different forms of media (gesture, speech, writing, image, and embodied performance) generate meaning for Indigenous groups; second, I am interested in how these relational media shift relations of power between settler and Indigenous rhetors; third, I focus on how particular forms of Indigenous expression such as Southern Plains Pictography or Plains Sign Talk generate intertribal relations that, in turn, generate new possibilities for collective action; finally, I delineate a relational practice for scholarly work in the archive that attends to positionality, spatiality, and responsibility such that Indigenous rhetorics can emerge in opposition to the settler institutions (colleges and universities, libraries, federal archives, special collections, and historical societies) that seek to contain them.

Indigenous rhetorics materialize from common experiences of colonization but also from a common relationship with and orientation to the lands of the American continent. Andrea Riley Mukavetz and Malea Powell (2015, 140–141) have argued that Indigenous practices of making arise from relations with the land, animals, and spirits who persist here: "This orientation to that set of relations, and the responsibilities that arise from maintaining 'right' relations, then forms the ambiguous boundaries of something we call Indigenous rhetorical practices." At Carlisle and Fort Marion, Indigenous rhetors developed communicative means to shift relations and reorient themselves to nation and land. These rhetorics emerge from the experience of the off-reservation boarding school as a particular site of colonial violence and intertribal connectivity. While one narrative of the boarding school experience is that of great trauma and loss, a coexisting story is one of Pan-Indian identity development and the incorporation of Euro-American literacy practices and technologies into the existing relations to land and language that Riley-Mukavetz and Powell describe. As Scott Richard Lyons has discussed, the narrative of the boarding school experience as trauma is so powerful that it has "colonized" even the memories of former students who did not themselves experience terrible abuses in school. Lyons (2010, 22) calls for "boarding schools to receive more complex treatment in the realm of public memory." I put forward the framework of a rhetoric of relations as a promising ground to explore what that complexity might look like.

This book demonstrates how a rhetoric of relations concretizes the workings of Indigenous rhetorics in the context of settler colonization, particularly in the period of heightened violence and coercion known as the Assimilation Era. Two key thinkers in Native American / Indigenous studies, Christopher Teuton (Cherokee) and Lisa Brooks (Abenaki), have theorized a relational framework for Indigenous communicative practices. For Teuton, oral, graphic, and critical impulses create balance between the affordances and drawbacks of each expressive form. He argues that oral discourses afford "a relational, experiential engagement with the world through sound-based forms of communication . . . they offer the potential for a more direct social engagement" (Teuton 2010, xvi). In contrast, graphic forms afford "the permanent recording of cultural knowledge in formats that will allow for recollection and study" (xvii). What Teuton terms the critical impulse "is always undercutting, always making messes, always disrupting things when they seem to be functioning well enough." The three impulses function in relation to ensure cultural survivance, which demands "a community's active engagement with the worldview its members continually construct" (xviii).

Lisa Brooks (2008, xxi) has argued similarly that Native writers "spin the binary between word and image into a relational framework," challenging the oppositional thinking through which settler scholars have long viewed communicative systems. *Precisely because* Indigenous rhetors construct stories in these relational media, their tactics are invisible to the Euro-American soldiers and teachers who decode language within a binary orality/literacy paradigm. *Precisely because* they draw on media that demand experiential engagement with the shifting conditions of the world, Indigenous rhetors persist in their expressive traditions by disrupting, shifting, and revising the communicative rules of assimilationist education.

A rhetoric of relations pushes back against the oral/literate divide that has characterized too much scholarship in rhetoric and composition. In other words, if settler scholars conceive of Indigenous Americans as only engaging history, memory, and story through oral practices, then we miss the embodied and material rhetorics that go hand in hand with oral modes. Counterintuitively, it is this very dichotomous thinking by settler teachers and scholars that allowed embodied and multimodal rhetorics to flourish in the boarding school system. Because settler teachers did not think of pictographic writing or Plains Sign Talk *as meaningful language*, they were unable to surveil, forbid, or punish these forms of tribal continuance. The archive allows us to glimpse student rhetorics beyond the alphabetic literacy forced upon them. When we learn to recognize and interpret these practices, we can better understand how Indigenous students drew upon the communicative reservoirs of their home cultures to survive boarding schools and create a future for Indigenous presence in the Americas.

NATIVE AMERICAN / INDIGENOUS STUDIES SPEAKS BACK TO RHETORIC AND COMPOSITION

This project follows in the footsteps of Scott Richard Lyons and Malea Powell, two scholars whose work demands that Indigenous worldviews hold a central position in any study of communication, persuasion, and writing in the American context. I have grappled with Lyons's term *rhetorical sovereignty*, what American Indians want from writing, and

Powell's "rhetorics of survivance," the *use* of writing by Native peoples, to make sense of Carlisle students' rhetorical tactics. These young people are barred in many ways from rhetorical sovereignty, "the inherent right and ability of *peoples* to determine their own communicative needs and desires . . . to decide for themselves the goals, modes, styles, and language of public discourse" (Lyons 2000, 449, original emphasis). Carlisle demanded that they give up the notion of peoplehood. Boarding schools aimed to detribalize, de-historicize, and reconstruct students' identities as English-literate subjects of the United States. And yet they did *use* writing, and like Sarah Winnemucca and Charles Eastman, their use of writing must be "seen as deliberately rhetorical, consciously and selectively interpretive with a specific audience's needs in mind" (Powell 2002, 406). In the chapters that follow, I read the texts of Native rhetors using their words and bodies to make meaning in the impossible rhetorical situation of assimilationist education.

Scholars have long viewed literacy as a contested site in the contact zone[4] between European and Indigenous cultures, yet Eurocentrism and settler-colonial fantasies continue to bear an undue and often invisible influence on literacy studies. European beliefs about writing historically privileged Western culture and justified the earliest colonial incursions into the Americas. As Stephen Greenblatt (2003, 9) has shown, Columbus and his contemporaries believed their "literal advantage" (the advantage of writing) connected them directly with God and conferred on them a unique ability to conceive of history. Centuries later, Great Divide proponents Eric Havelock, Jack Goody, and Walter Ong exemplify the powerful grip such colonizing beliefs retained into the twentieth century. In varying iterations, they proposed that literacy and orality create fundamentally different social conditions and that the literate side of this opposition carries more cultural and cognitive value.[5] When rhetoric and composition theorizes literacy and orality, then, we do so in ways that are fraught with colonial baggage. We have too often accepted and perpetuated the myths of Euro-American colonization that demand we un-see the literate and expressive forms of Indigenous nations.

Despite the growing presence of Native American and Indigenous scholars and scholarly approaches in literacy and rhetorical studies—exemplified by such thinkers as Malea Powell, Scott Lyons, Qwo-Li Driskill, Lisa King, Ellen Cushman, Emily Legg, Andrea Riley Mukavetz, Angela Haas, and others—colonial views of literacy continue to restrict the accuracy and scope of analysis in a number of historically focused fields. Alyssa Mt. Pleasant, Caroline Wigginton, and Kelly Wisecup (2018, 417) argue that the beliefs of the continent's first colonists continue to restrict the materials and methods used by today's scholars:

> Colonists' emphasis on alphabetic literacy and insistence that trustworthy history take written forms continue to orient both historiographical practices and conceptions of the literary, despite the ongoing importance of oral traditions and nonalphabetic materials for Native authors and communities . . . allowing genres such as the captivity narrative, novel, and sermon and forms of literacy such as alphabetic writing to orient our literary histories can silence Indigenous literary and intellectual histories while leaving to the side or framing through colonial categories the diverse media and oratorical practices on which native people drew.

Given the fraught role (mis)understandings of Indigenous expressive traditions play in the fields of literary, historical, and rhetorical studies, this book focuses on the wide range of embodied, textual, and graphic forms boarding school students engaged as well as how those forms were rendered invisible or illegible to the colonial gaze.

To address the ongoing limitations of settler-colonial mythos in studies of literacy and rhetoric, I rely heavily on John Duffy's notion of "rhetorics of literacy," a concept that carves a path forward from the faulty premises of the Great Divide thesis. Duffy (2007, 60) maligns the binary of literacy and orality as a "twentieth-century expression of the nineteenth-century tradition of anthropology." A rhetorics of literacy methodology defines the two key terms at play in the following interrelated way: *rhetoric* is "the ways of using language and other symbols by institutions, groups, or individuals for the purpose of shaping concepts of reality," and *literacy* is the technical contrivance through which that concept of reality moves through the world (15). Because Indigenous expressive traditions so frequently fall under the mischaracterizations of colonial audiences such as ethnographers, anthropologists, and educational reformers, rhetorics of literacy is an ideal framework for the type of situated and historicized work I am engaging here. We can begin to ask, what social beliefs and political agendas underlie curricular decisions? What motives prompt teachers to reward some communicative modes while pathologizing others? What global systems are implicated in institutional norms? Literacy does not exist outside of the personal, cultural, institutional, transnational, historical, or rhetorical realms Duffy has identified (193–200). To understand the Carlisle school language curriculum is to make sense of the complex web of forces that made Indigenous language eradication possible.

This book traces how meaning was constructed and negotiated within the Carlisle school itself but also within the various publics the school aimed to influence. These publics include the Protestant religious and missionary organizations that called themselves the "Friends of the Indian," agents and bureaucrats of the federal government, Indigenous leaders and collectives, as well as a wide swath of the Euro-American public interested in Indian policy and Indian education after the Indian Wars on the Southern Plains. Indigenous and Euro-American rhetors also addressed internal audiences made up of Fort Marion prisoners and jailers and, later, Carlisle authorities and students. These competing rhetors deployed strategies in print, graphic, and embodied media to impose their worldviews on one another and shift the field of power relations in which they interacted. Indigenous rhetors drew upon what K. Tsianina Lomawaima (1994, xiii) calls "the markers of identity inherited from home and learned at the school—tribal background, language, degree of blood, physical appearance"—to reconstitute their orientations and audiences as tribal ways of life came under new forms of attack. The rhetorical history traced in the following pages demonstrates how the colonial scene is one of persuasion, where meaning comes unhinged from existing tethers for both colonizer and colonized. New possibilities for inter- and intra-cultural relations emerge as both groups adapt to one another's communicative technologies. Revising such expressive traditions as Plains Sign Talk, pictographic writing, embodied performances of bravery and self-sacrifice, and strategic engagements with print, Fort Marion prisoners and Carlisle students showed that Indigenous rhetorical traditions would not disappear beneath the imperative of assimilation.

Because I am invested in unsettling the ongoing and tacit conception of a single, Euro-Western rhetorical tradition, I draw centrally on scholarship in Native American / Indigenous studies to engage with the multiple, competing, and equally rich rhetorical traditions that come into contact through settler-colonialism in the Americas. I borrow the term *expressive tradition(s)* from Mt. Pleasant, Wigginton, and Wisecup (2018). I appreciate the term in its capaciousness and use it as an umbrella concept to demarcate the various textual and extra-textual (i.e., oral, performative, material, embodied) practices deployed by Indigenous Americans within their rhetorical repertoires. My focus on the communicative world of the Americas is a deliberate one that grounds the experiences of students at off-reservation boarding schools within the history of both colonization and Indigenous cultural productions before and in opposition to that colonization. In this sense, my project follows Damían Baca's (2010, 3) call for rhetorical histories that account for how Indigenous artists and writers have "responded and continue to respond to imperialist teleology and Western expansion." By studying the workings of Indigenous rhetorics under the particular historical conditions of assimilation, I demonstrate how Indigenous cultural resilience emerges from their communicative practices, particularly the elasticity of those practices and their ability to change over time.

This project is indebted to recent scholarship that places Indigenous literary, historicist, graphic, and material expressive forms at the center of scholarly inquiry. As Birgit Brander Rasmussen (2014, 259) has argued, colonial techniques such as the destruction of historical documents and limiting scholarly definitions of literacy work to make Native American writing systems invisible to settlers and settler scholars. In the past decade, research on media, cultures of print, and book history has led to a rich body of work on Indigenous communicative techniques beyond the written word.[6] The work of this volume is to join this conversation with new insights into how the body enters Indigenous expressive action in relation to graphic and written forms. My goal is to further our understanding of how relational rhetorics reverberate in the graphic, material, and textual documentary history that is readily available in nineteenth-century archives.

The body has a fraught history in rhetorical studies and an equally fraught history in scientific racism of the nineteenth century. Karma R. Chávez (2018, 242) has articulated how the body serves as both an "abstract and actual rhetorical concept" in rhetorical studies. At times, this book approaches the body from each angle. First, I am interested in how Native American/Indigenous bodies were racialized at Fort Marion and Carlisle and in the nineteenth-century settler imagination. I discuss shifting theories of race and their impact on curriculum at Carlisle in chapter 2. In this sense, this book conceives of the "Indian" body as an abstraction that is imagined to have fixed biological or cultural differences from the Euro-American body. Part of the racialization of Native Americans in the Assimilation Era involved conceiving of the Indian as culturally disabled in relation to the imagined "advanced" US culture. As Siobhan Senier (2012) has argued, attributing disability to Indigenous peoples is a tool for resource extraction: "Once Indigenous people have been pathologized, labeled 'the Indian problem,' the path is clear for colonial exploitation. Native dis-ability means that they are unable to manage their own resources—their children, their trees and game, their uranium. Native mortality means that their land is available for the taking." The Carlisle school is a chilling example of how US government policy generated Native disability materially (through institutional diseases like tuberculosis, pneumonia, and trachoma) and discursively (by pathologizing Native languages and cultures). To understand how the Indigenous body came to be viewed as disabled and in need of institutional intervention, I interrogate how—to borrow from Duffy (2007, 15)—rhetoric is reality shaping. In the Assimilation Era, the rhetoric of Indians disabled by their culture generated massive institutional energy for the reform of reservation life and Indian education. Racialized beliefs led settler military and educational workers to surveil, control, incarcerate, attire, and otherwise violently interact with Indigenous bodies at Fort Marion and Carlisle.

How Indigenous rhetors reacted to that violence demonstrates the ways the body can be a "vehicle for rhetorical performance" and "an often ignored but important site of rhetorical invention" (Chávez 2018, 243). When I put forward a rhetoric of relations, I mean to create a framework that conveys not only the rich repository of meaningful embodied acts Fort Marion prisoners and Carlisle students performed but also the ways other expressive traditions document those meaningful embodied acts. A good example appears in chapter 1, where I read Etahdleuh Doanmoe's Fort Marion sketchbook not as the story of his journey from savagery to civilization (which is Richard Pratt's interpretation and the reason he treasured and preserved the text) but rather as a graphic history of the embodied resistance of Doanmoe's fellow prisoners. I argue that the sketchbook subversively reproduces the suicide and escape attempts undertaken by other members of his intertribal group of captives. The sketchbook, then, represents not an enclosed documentary history itself but a historical text working *in relation* with Kiowa oral histories. These subtle sketches of suicide attempts or violence against the guards would be made legible in oral re-tellings of the pictographic text yet remain invisible within the Euro-American jailers' interpretive frameworks. Embodied actions and experiences enter the documentary record again and again in these archives, serving as sites of resistance when alphabetic literacy itself was a tool of coercion and surveillance.

At off-reservation boarding schools, educators scrutinized and surveilled the bodies of the Native students. According to Pratt (1964, 2), students would not be able to learn English until their bodies were appropriately de-indigenized. He wrote in early 1880, "The daily [English] sessions were short, and not much was effected until blankets had disappeared." As long as the children wore markers of their tribes on their bodies, Pratt was sure they could not learn English. As Penelope Kelsey (2013, 199) argues, "While the physical conformity of Indigenous bodies was sought most immediately, the minds of pupils were the ultimate site of contestation." In this way, an embodied set of codes and norms preceded English-language training. Jay Dolmage (2014, 4) calls this phenomenon the "rhetorical push-and-pull [of disability] not just wherever we might recover disabled bodies, but also when we find any supposedly 'abnormal' body—foreign, raced, feminized, sexualized, diseased, aging." Indigenous bodies became abnormal to justify policies of assimilation.[7]

This book views the body as both a site of trauma and racialization *and* a site of individual, tribal, and intertribal survivance at Fort Marion and the Carlisle school. Cutcha Risling Baldy articulates the importance of the body as a medium for survivance in her recent work on Hupa women's coming-of-age ceremonies. Following the "violent and repeated violations of Native children through inappropriate surveillance and also physical violations of their bodies" at boarding school, Risling Baldy (2018, 15, 21) discusses the revitalization of coming-of-age ceremonies as a type of "embodied decolonization." The following chapters suggest that even within the constraints of the military prison and the boarding school, prisoners and students took part in processes of embodied decolonization that built resilience within these spaces and carved out a path for emergent intertribal movements of cultural revitalization and self-determination in the twentieth century and beyond.

A RELATIONAL PRACTICE IN THE ARCHIVE

When I enter spaces to engage with documentary evidence of the Carlisle school, I do so as a white woman teacher, following the path of other white women teachers who came before me. In many ways, this archive is familiar. In many ways, this collection of documents is intended for me. As many readers will know, the work of teaching and administration creates reams of documents that make little sense to those outside a particular institution's walls. These texts emerge from the immediate exigencies of running a school or managing a classroom. Richard Pratt created another layer of institutional memory when he invited photographer John Choate to document the activities and faces of his pupils; even these images are familiar to me as an education worker. Through such evidence as photographs, worksheets, reports, and letters, institutions tell stories about themselves. These stories are collective, bureaucratic fabrications that reproduce the institution and its values across time and space. Settler institutions of the nineteenth century were obsessed with the posterity of their stories. The repositories of these stories are very sturdy. They have thick walls and dry vaults. They have folders and boxes and acid-free paper. These stories live on in the Cumberland County Historical Society and the Dickinson College Special Collections. They live in the National Archives in Washington, DC, where you can find hundreds of letters exchanged between the US Indian Bureau and Richard Pratt. These stories live in memorial plaques around the city of Carlisle and on the grounds of the Army War College, even in the cemetery of students who died at Carlisle, which has been relocated to the very edge of the active army base today. Settler forms of documentation reflect settler beliefs about language, history, and memory. The privileged position of alphabetic literacy is made clear. Anything written down on paper is more likely to be preserved. The settler society justifies our presence through the sheer volume of words we have written on the lands of the American continent. It is as though documentation of assimilationist efforts proves that assimilation occurred.

To understand this archive, I have looked closely at both the bureaucratic and photographic documentation of these institutions. Each type of text tells a part of the story. Lessons appear on chalk boards in the backgrounds of classroom photographs, on photographs of slates, in annual reports. I find a collection of student math problems: "If one bar of soap costs three cents, how many will you get for fifteen cents?" I find lists of books in expense reports sent to the US Indian Bureau for approval. I find photographs of students sitting at their desks or marching around the grounds or laboring in the tin shop and the print shop. I read about sewing lessons and a reading room where children can find English-language periodicals to read in their limited free time. Each of these elements tells part of the story.

Amid the boxes and folders and PDFs of student newspapers, the process of making meaning is daunting. I find this process best theorized by E. Cram (2016, 111) as *archival ambience*: "how archival environments act as a medium that orients bodies, feelings, and sensations relative to their memorializing contexts." Cram illuminates how queering the archive involves a practice of positionality and relationality. In their words, "The relationality of archival ambience generates a landscape of feeling, and affectability begets conditions for archival invention" (115). Developing a relational practice demands that I contend with my own affectability in the archive of this settler institution. Unlike Malea Powell (2008, 117), who has written about her experience as "an Indian talking about what it means to be an Indian in the archive, what it means to be the object looking back, the objectified engaged in the process of making knowledge about the processes that led to my objectification," I find myself all too comfortable amid the detritus of old English lessons. I realize that these teachers are no so different from myself. I, too, write reports to document learning outcomes. I, too, engage in quotidian bureaucratic writing. I, too, negotiate the standardizing influences of institutions when I read and respond to my students' written work. Barring a critical, de-colonial praxis, my work would not be so different from that of these teachers whose documentary evidence has been preserved for posterity.

All of this is to say that my archival practice is constrained by the realities of settler-colonial institutions, epistemologies, and technologies of inscription and memory. As such, I approach the Carlisle archive with great humility, not to determine what *did* happen but, in the vein of Jacqueline Jones Royster's (Royster and Kirsch 2012, 71) concept of *critical imagination*, "what might likely be true based on what we have in hand." And I am not critically imagining alone. Scholarship in Native American / Indigenous studies provides a powerful set of methodologies and interpretive frameworks to reread Indigenous media that has made its way into imperial archives. I am thinking of Stephanie Fitzgerald's (2008) reading of Mohegan history as inscribed on a painted basket or Marge Bruchac's work on repatriating wampum belts to the communities whose history is inscribed therein. I am thinking of Ellen Cushman's (2011) excellent book on the Cherokee syllabary, where she explores how Cherokee cosmologies, epistemologies, and sovereignty inhere within the syllabary itself.[8] When I work in the Carlisle archive, these methodologies teach me how to interpret students' writing, students' embodied practices, and the graphic media in which students inscribed their stories.

As I move and think through the documents that have been assembled in colonial edifices such as the Dickinson College Special Collections, the Cumberland County Historical Society, Yale's Beinecke Library, and the US National Archives, I acknowledge my responsibility to chronicle not only the stories of Indigenous rhetors but also the stories of the teachers and administrators who abused their power and understood that abuse through myths of their own benevolence. My aim is to bring to light the legacy of colonial violence that lives within the practice of teaching English while also revisiting the texts and performances of students who faced that violence. As Powell (2008, 121) articulates, the archival scholar is responsible for remembering that archival materials are not "simply available objects; no, they are alive, and their harvest requires the appropriate gestures of respect, friendship, honor, and good will." These gestures work against the imperial impulse toward salvage ethnography and theft that has led museums and archives to hold sacred, cultural, and historical materials away from the Indigenous nations for whom they are a vital part of life and memory. I also take seriously Gesa Kirsch's (Royster and Kirsch 2012, viii) insight that "archival records are never simply transparent. Just as a collection of records is established from an interested perspective, it is also read from an interested perspective." Emily Legg, too, has argued that our material histories "are also value laden because they were 'worth' archiving." As such, archival scholars must redirect the values and impulses behind colonial practices of collection and preservation. Legg (2014, 73) insists that "we must begin by undoing the practice of unseeing, especially writing practices and educational models of underrepresented peoples." We only have access to the Fort Marion and Carlisle materials because Richard Pratt and his cohorts maintained careful records as part of their bureaucratic responsibilities to the federal government. Carlisle materials were read and collected to document the imagined end of Indigenous life in America and necessarily limit our full understanding of students' rhetorics of survivance.

Following Powell, Kirsch, and Legg, I insist that there are ways to engage the Carlisle archive that lend powerful insight into the workings of Indigenous rhetoric and resistance. As Jacqueline Emery (2017, 5) asserts in her recent edited collection of boarding school texts, "Boarding school newspapers are an untapped archive for scholars working to recover early Indigenous writings and to challenge the restrictive assimilationist-resistance binary that has dominated narratives of the boarding school experience." Scholars are increasingly reading these periodicals against and beyond their assimilationist performances to better understand how students developed "tricky and subtle" strategies of critique (13). By revisiting student texts that are uncomfortably aligned with the boarding school philosophy, my own project extends our understandings of Native American writing in the Assimilation Era. More important, however, I am interested in how students conceived of and enacted survivance through their engagement with and revision of their nations' expressive traditions. I argue that no archival study can look at alphabetic writing alone to capture the strategies of these students. Embodied, graphic, and material rhetorics exist all over this archive and illuminate how students were always exploring their English-language learning in relation to their existing repertoires.

Diana Taylor uses the term *repertoire* in contrast to "archive," and part of my work here is to bring these two terms into relation. For Taylor (2003, 19), the archive "exists as documents, maps, literary texts, letters, archaeological remains, bones, videos, films, cds, all those items supposedly resistant to change." The repertoire, in contrast, "enacts embodied memory: performances, gestures, orality, movement, dance, singing—in short, all those acts usually thought of as ephemeral, nonreproducible knowledge" (20). Taylor is attuned to how culture travels and changes through ephemeral acts with bounded temporalities and audiences. I contend that the Fort Marion and Carlisle archive demonstrates how the archive and the repertoire act in concert to create forms of memory that may only be legible to cultural insiders with an interest in retaining the secrecy of their communal knowledge. I am thinking of the many ways embodied performances enter this archive, such as how Etahdleuh Doanmoe captures the ephemeral, embodied acts of bravery that Cheyenne chiefs Gray Beard and Lean Bear perform on their journey from Fort Sill to Fort Marion. Or how Ernest White Thunder's hunger strike and death enter and shape the written record through letters, petitions, x-marks, nonfiction, and treaty negotiations decades after his embodied acts. These performances accrue meaning not only for their immediate audiences but also for broader publics that emerge and shift due to colonial conditions of the late nineteenth century. When I say that hunger striking or running away reverberates in the print public sphere, I am talking about how the archive of preserved, written texts is not a static form of memory. This is memory that evolves as political possibilities change for Indigenous peoples in their ongoing fight for self-determination and the end to settler colonization.

As conditions of possibility change, so, too, does the meaning of the archive. I make sense of the shifting political implications of the Carlisle archive in Ann Cvetkovich's (2003, 7) formulation of an archive of feelings—"an exploration of cultural texts as repositories of feelings and emotions, which are encoded not only in the content of the texts but in practices that surround their production and reception." For Cvetkovich, trauma challenges how we think about archives by putting "pressure on conventional forms of documentation, representation, and commemoration, giving rise to new genres of expression, such as testimony, and new forms of monuments, rituals, and performances that can call into being collective witnesses and publics" (7). While Cvetkovich comes to the concept through her study of lesbian performances and engagements with queer trauma, I find her work particularly helpful in understanding how Carlisle students and Fort Marion prisoners encoded their stories in ways that would reverberate in public decoding processes long after their experiences of incarceration. Prisoners at Fort Marion and students in Carlisle's first years are undoubtedly experiencing unprecedented forms of trauma, and this impacts how they encode their experiences. In some cases, these rhetors take genres from their national traditions into new spaces, using Plains Sign Talk on the Carlisle campus or creating pictographic histories with colored pencils and paper instead of buffalo hide and paint. In other cases, they develop new genres of expression such as running away or using stories of their bodies to encode their traumatic experiences into periodical print. In still other cases, these rhetors perform ceremonies such as the Sun Dance in entirely new ways to gesture toward a return to good relations with their communities even though they cannot communicate with their relatives in their homelands. These forms of embodied and material expression build a future when there will be new possibilities beyond the constraints of the moment. In this sense, Fort Marion and Carlisle documentary evidence can be assembled into an "archive of feelings" that generates the conditions of possibility for intertribal and sovereign publics of Indigenous resistors into the twentieth century and beyond.

The following chapters approach the early years of the Assimilation Era through close attention to archival and periodical documents related to the Carlisle Indian School. Chapter 1 examines the archive of relational rhetorics deployed by Fort Marion prisoners as they aimed to construct the futurity of their nations on the shifting ground of settler colonization. I argue that Fort Marion prisoners engaged in a rhetoric of relations to make settler violence visible even as settler rhetoric insisted on US national innocence. These prisoners also engaged in performances of personal sacrifice for the benefit of the group, both for their immediate audience of fellow prisoners and their communities in their homelands. This chapter focuses on how individual prisoners recognized that while they may not have had a future as individuals, their texts, their communities, and their homelands did. This is the story the Fort Marion prisoners tell in media ranging from pictographic sketches to the Sun Dance ceremony to suicide.

Chapter 2 weaves through logics of language, race, and disability in the Assimilation Era and how these competing and overlapping logics impacted the earliest Carlisle language and literacy curriculum. Indigenous students' use of Plains Sign Talk (PST) serves as a grounding case study in how Indian languages were interpreted by educational reformers and how that interpretation impacted everyday lessons. In an extraordinary feat of un-seeing Indigenous literacies, Pratt based his English-only curriculum on the assumption that Indians and the deaf would benefit from an identical, gesture-based approach. This interpretation of PST had far-reaching effects for pedagogy and curriculum at Carlisle. But as in all cases throughout this book, Plains Sign Talk remained a powerful rhetoric of relations and resistance as Pratt and his contemporaries (mis)interpreted this language as evidence of Indigenous cultural disability.

Chapter 3 examines the embodied rhetorics of a student named Ernest White Thunder within the larger context of Lakota refusal of allotment policies of the 1880s. Ernest was among the first group of students to come to Carlisle from the Sicangu Oyate, or Burnt Thigh Nation, at the Rosebud Agency in South Dakota. He entered school at age eighteen and went on a hunger strike to resist the curriculum and his captivity away from his homeland. This chapter pushes back against the notion of rhetoric as a set of persuasive communicative strategies to most expediently bring about a desired result. Rather, drawing on the work of Audra Simpson, I argue that an Indigenous rhetoric of relations is not expedient. It is better understood as "the phenomenon of people thinking and acting as nationals in a scene of dispossession" (Simpson 2014, 33). Ernest White Thunder refused to abandon his national identity in the face of overwhelming colonial pressure, and he used his body to communicate that refusal when all other forms of resistance failed. In so doing, he modeled a rhetoric of refusal that would ignite further refusals by members of his nation as they came to terms with the deaths of their children and how the boarding school project fit within larger settler-colonial tactics to dispossess the Lakota of their land.

Chapter 4 turns to students who did not explicitly reject the curriculum for assimilation they encountered at Carlisle but who molded their rhetorical tactics in ways that blended alphabetic and embodied forms to envision new ways for their nations to exist in the Assimilationist Era. While previous chapters focus primarily on embodied rhetorical forms such as Plains Sign Talk or hunger striking, chapter 4 looks at how students wrote about their bodies in Carlisle's periodical press, creating a relational rhetoric of body and text. In so doing, they registered their resistance while also meeting the demands of their first and most critical audience—their teachers. Because students were so limited in what they could say—punished for speaking in their own language, humiliated for making mistakes in English—and even more limited in what they could write, I argue that students used their bodies to circulate meaning among their peers, with their distant families, and with their unknown but imagined Euro-American readers.

The book closes with a brief discussion of the legacy of Carlisle and how the school's visual culture has found new purchase in an era when once again the federal government is taking children away from their families to achieve the goal of a monoculture coterminous with the territorial boundaries of the nation-state. By looking at the many ways we see Carlisle in our contemporary rhetorical environments, I argue for the necessity of a relational framework for interpreting Indigenous rhetoric, from the textual to the graphic, material, performative, or embodied. The political purchase gained by remixed, revised, and repurposed Carlisle materials demonstrates the power of Indigenous rhetoric to continue challenging the myth of American innocence while opening new possibilities for a future beyond the limited imagination of the settler state.

1

PLAINS PICTOGRAPHY AND EMBODIED RESISTANCE AT FORT MARION

Following the Buffalo War of 1874–1875, Plains nations found their life-ways decimated. Buffalo were integral to life for the Kiowa, Cheyenne, and other Plains tribes, so when federal troops slaughtered herds to the point of near extinction, starvation and exhaustion led to a series of captures and surrenders by these nations at Fort Sill (what is currently Oklahoma) (Earenfight 2007a, 12). As Kiowa writer N. Scott Momaday (Momaday and Momaday 1998, 1) explains, "The buffalo was the animal representation of the sun, the essential sacrificial victim of the Sun Dance. When the wild herds were destroyed, so too was the will of the Kiowa people." A fragile peace agreement between tribal leaders and the US Department of War stipulated that thirty-three Cheyenne, twenty-seven Kiowa, nine Comanche, two Arapaho, and one Caddo warrior were to be exiled indefinitely to Fort Marion in St. Augustine, Florida (Earenfight 2007a, 17). On April 28, 1875, the men were shackled and put in wagons with Black Horse's daughter Ah-kes and wife, Pe-ah-in, who jumped into his wagon as the caravan departed to begin the 1,000-mile journey east (Glancy 2014, 2). Also imprisoned was a Cheyenne woman, Mo-chi, or Buffalo Calf Woman, who was charged with striking a white man on the head with an ax (Mann 1997, 40). On May 21, the caravan arrived in Florida and Richard Henry Pratt began his program of education in military training and English literacy. He cut the prisoners' hair, dressed them in military uniforms, and brought in local schoolteachers to give literacy lessons. The prisoners lived in small cells, called casemates. During the first few months, they only saw the sky from the courtyard at the center of the fort.

Two years later, Pratt had gained fame for civilizing the savage warriors. Fort Marion drew the attention of social reformers including Harriet Beecher Stowe, who visited St. Augustine in the spring of 1877. She wrote about the visit for the *Christian Union*, describing a prison service where she observed a prayer led by the Cheyenne elder Minimic:

DOI: 10.7330/9781646420872.c001

The sound of the prayer was peculiarly mournful. Unused to the language, we could not discriminate words: it seemed a succession of moans, of imploring wails; it was what the Bible so often speaks of in relation to prayer, a "cry" unto God; in it we seemed to hear all the story of the wrongs, the cruelties, the injustice which had followed these children of the forest, driving them to wrong and cruelty in return. (Stowe 1877, 372)

In her re-telling, Stowe displays long-held settler beliefs about Indians. She conjures what can only be described as Minimic's noble savagery, a trope that Philip J. Deloria (1998, 4) argues "both juxtaposes and conflates an urge to idealize and desire Indians and a need to despise and dispossess them." The Indians prisoners are incomprehensible to Stowe, but their worship harkens back to a primitive, Old Testament appeal to God. They are victims. They are children who should have been protected by a benevolent, paternal American nation and instead were harmed. They have been led astray by the cruelty of the colonial power. The phrase "children of the forest" comes from a nineteenth-century literary tradition of proclaiming the inevitable disappearance of Indian nations. Stowe draws upon such writers as James Fenimore Cooper, Henry Wadsworth Longfellow, and Lydia Maria Child with her rhetoric of childlike and noble Indians who need to be protected and educated by the US government.

But there are no forests on the Southern Plains, and these are prisoners of war, not children. The men held at Fort Marion experience the post-bellum iteration of what Deloria (1998, 5) calls "a two-hundred-year back-and-forth between assimilation and destruction." Finding themselves caught between these two impossible options, they perform Indian identity to appease their captors. According to Stowe, Minimic turns to his Euro-American audience after the prayer to translate. He tells his white audience that "they thanked the Great Spirit that he had shown them a new road, a better way; opened their eyes to see and their ears to hear. They wanted to go again to their own land, to see their wives and children and to teach them the better way" (Stowe 1877, 372). Even as Stowe attempts to map the prisoners into her conceptual framework of noble savagery, the prisoners retain a collective voice as they push back, demanding that their captors recognize their petition to return to their homelands. Their incarceration represents a particularly cruel and arbitrary action on the part of the US government because "from the Cheyenne perspective . . . banishment or isolation was the sentence for intratribal murder, the most extreme . . . behavior in their social structure. Thus, symbolically this separation sundered their very social fabric" (Mann 1997, 40–41). As I argue throughout this chapter, these demands enter the colonial discourse through Plains rhetorical traditions that prisoners adapt to address their changing circumstances. That is, when Minimic performs at a Christian prayer service, he does so in his own language and then strategically translates his speech into a petition. Fighting to preserve the Cheyenne territory is the very reason Minimic and his fellow prisoners are captives. His speech advances ongoing Cheyenne campaigns to maintain their ancestral territory.

The rest of Stowe's article describes how the prisoners have learned to value industry and given up their nomadic ways. She argues for a new national commitment to Indian education to prevent further bloodshed. She praises the prisoners for wanting to farm, blacksmith, and bake bread. She references Japanese students attending the Amherst State Agricultural School (now the University of Massachusetts Amherst) as a model for the cultural education the Indian men might pursue after their captivity. Stowe's brief essay is prophetic of the shifting role of education in American imperialism. Shortly following the publication of this piece, Colonel Richard Henry Pratt opened the Carlisle Indian Industrial School, which introduced the English-only paradigm to Native children from New England to Alaska. Even Puerto Rican and Filipino children were subject to Pratt's English-only program following the Spanish-American War. The Fort Marion prisoners experienced the earliest form of this paradigm shift, and for that reason, the rhetorical history of the Carlisle school begins here.

This chapter looks at the rhetoric of relations deployed by Fort Marion prisoners as they work to demonstrate their futurity on the shifting rhetorical ground of settler colonization. As the Fort Marion prisoners and, later, the Carlisle students demonstrate, Native nations are not fading away or growing out of their indigeneity through education. They are present and will continue to be present long after the scourge of European settler colonization has ended. The relational rhetorics of Fort Marion prisoners make material Indigenous corporality and futurity by engaging what Beth Piatote (2013, 9) has called "an anticolonial imaginary: visions of alternative futures that may explain, in part, how Indian communities survived the violence of the assimilation era." The Fort Marion prisoners make visible the violence of Pratt and the US government. They engage in performances of personal sacrifice for the benefit of the group. The individual prisoners may not have a future, but their texts, their communities, and their land bases do. This is the story Minimic and his fellow prisoners tell in media ranging from pictographic sketches to the Sun Dance rituals to suicide attempts. Most important, this is a story about the affordances of relational rhetorics of the Southern Plains and how those rhetorical traditions allowed the prisoners at Fort Marion to resist their captivity while preserving their stories for the future use of their nations.

FROM SAVAGE TO STUDENT: RHETORICAL CONSTRUCTIONS OF THE INDIAN IN THE ASSIMILATION ERA   .

Richard Henry Pratt is recognized as the founder of the off-reservation boarding school movement, but his experiences in Indian education actually began at Fort Marion in 1875. He was tasked with holding seventy-two prisoners from the Southern Plains for an indefinite period. In his autobiography, Pratt suggests that his model for Indian education emerged out of circumstance and improvisation; he implemented military-style discipline and English-literacy education to both control and occupy the prisoners during their incarceration. Alongside his laissez-faire narrative about the invention of a model for assimilationist education, however, Pratt begins to articulate the larger context that guided his actions. Pratt saw himself as an advocate for justice. He wanted to bring about "the rights of citizenship including fraternity and equal privilege for development" of the Indian (Utley 1964, xi). He felt that reservations unjustly segregated Native Americans and kept them from entering into the social goods enjoyed by US citizens. Underlying these moral claims is also a shifting approach to Indian affairs in the federal government. As allotment policies gained traction, Pratt's moral stance against Indian segregation resonated with the federal government's desire to break up reservation land and open further territory for resource extraction and settlement. Like so many language and literacy educators, Pratt worked within a fantasy of benevolence. He viewed his role as separate and distinct from the settler project of resource acquisition and upheld that view by constructing a trope of the Indian to fit a new age of settler colonization.

The figure of the Indian student was not new. In fact, it drew its particular power from building on long-held tropes of the Indian in US cultural productions. In American literary and legal texts, Native Americans are figured as noble savages, disappearing Indians, children of the forest, domestic dependent nations, and, at the end of the nineteenth century, students. As Jean O'Brien (2010, xxi) has argued, these tropes engage a temporality that holds Native peoples outside of modernity. The noble savage is pre-modern. The disappearing Indian vanishes to avoid becoming modern. The domestic dependent nation, a concept articulated in the 1831 *Cherokee Nation v. Georgia* decision, posits that the

Cherokee cannot become modern as sovereign nationals but must enter modernity as childlike dependents of more advanced settler citizens. The ruling also places tribal political organizations "in a state of pupilage," confining Indigenous peoples to a student-like status in relation to their benefactor, the United States (Piatote 2013, 5). The Indian student is related to these earlier tropes (as a perpetual child, for example), but this is a youth who can learn to approximate European cultural maturity. The Indian as student acts as a convenient figure to justify policies of forced assimilation.

The Indian as student was particularly suited to colonial desires of the late nineteenth century when the end to the Civil War created an increased demand for national unity, a tension that had historically been eased by moving the frontier ever-westward to open land and resources to disaffected whites.[1] By rhetoric here I follow John Duffy's (2007, 15) definition: "the ways of using language and other symbols by institutions, groups, or individuals for the purpose of shaping concepts of reality." Rhetorical theory is a crucial and underutilized lens to understand how literacy, media, and education reinforce settler-colonial dominance. Under settler-colonialism, the moral authority of the settler state must be shored up by the unremitting obfuscation of a simple fact: settlers occupy a land base to which they have no historical claim. Scholars of literature, American history, and performance studies have done excellent work in delineating how this obfuscation happens in novels, poems, the legal system, and diplomatic ceremonies. And yet, rhetoric has not been fully embraced to make sense of the persuasive nature of intercultural contact in the Americas—the ways encounters between settler and Indigenous peoples play out as a negotiation of cultural and military dominance. Nor have we fully considered how intercultural communication in colonial encounters is embodied. As Jay Dolmage (2014, 5) has argued, "We should recognize rhetoric as the circulation of discourse through the body." In the day-to-day negotiation of power, culture, and control at Fort Marion, assimilation and resistance were embodied processes. Rhetoric lends insight into how bodies make meaning. Through rhetoric, we can interrogate the paracolonial sites of the military prison and the boarding school (see Vizenor 1994, 77).

Fort Marion and Carlisle also illuminate how myths of Indian identity permeated the public sphere of the United States in the nineteenth century, making new forms of colonial violence not only imaginable but justifiable as well. Eve Tuck and Wayne Yang (2012, 9) have delineated common settler moves to innocence: myths or tropes that enable "a settler desire to be made innocent, to find some mercy or relief in [the] face of the relentlessness of settler guilt and haunting." The figure of Indian as student certainly falls within this framework and demonstrates how settlers in the late nineteenth century wished to absolve themselves of colonial guilt while pushing forward ever-accelerating forms of domination and land theft. I would argue that settler moves to innocence are best understood as rhetorical—that is, persuasive—invested in defining reality in terms that benefit settler-colonialism. As Lisa King (2015, 25) has argued, constructions of Indians and savagism work as Burkean terministic screens through which non-Native communities function. During the Plains Wars, settler culture constructed the Indian as a violent savage who presented an existential threat to the United States. For Pratt, the Indian was not inherently evil, only hindered by his culture and language. Pratt amplified the trope of Indian as student of civilization to replace the trope of Indian as violent, savage warrior, but both terministic screens have the same effect: the murder and dispossession of Indigenous peoples. If Indians were savage warriors, they could be killed in war as enemy combatants. If Indians were students learning to be fully American, then their language, kinship, and land rights were as malleable as their uncultivated minds. Unlike treaty agreements that posited two equal nations in diplomatic relations, the Indian as student figure allowed the US government to circumvent existing treaty arrangements in the name of well-meaning paternalism. In this way, the fantasy of benevolence engaged by literacy educators became a colonial tactic working in concert with more explicitly violent forms of domination.

The Indian as student was compatible with perhaps the most persistent myth in the settler imaginary: the disappearing Indian. The boarding school movement promised a new type of disappearance; rather than fading naturally and willingly into the Western wilderness as Chingachgook does in James Fenimore Cooper's novel *The Last of the Mohicans*, these Indians will disappear through education. This new iteration of the disappearing Indian myth served to justify new forms of US colonial violence—it was the dysfunctional and anachronistic culture of the Indian that led to his fading presence on the land, not the slaughter of peoples and buffalo on the Southern Plains. Gerald Vizenor (1994, ix) has theorized Indians such as Chingachgook as "immovable simulations, the tragic archives of dominance and victimry." These Indians are represented and reproduced through manifest manners, the "racialist notions and misnomers sustained in archives and lexicons as 'authentic' representations of *indian* cultures" (vii). Through the concept of manifest manners, Vizenor has articulated how language shores up settler colonialism. The primary mechanism of that shoring up is the static and unchanging Indian who loses his claim to nation, land, and language by deviating from settler perceptions of the traditional, static, and authentic. Pratt's vision of the Indian student was a late nineteenth-century iteration of these manifest manners.

Pratt propagated the myth of the static, authentic, and disappearing Indian by obsessively chronicling the cultures and bodies of his prisoners. He took pains to photograph them in their tribal attire upon arrival at Fort Marion, encouraged them to perform dances for St. Augustine audiences, copied and translated a pictographic letter written by Manimic[2] for posterity, and solicited sculptor Clark Mills to come from Washington, DC, to make life casts of the Indians' heads for preservation and scientific study at the Smithsonian Institution (Glancy 2014, 38).[3] Philip Deloria (1998, 90) has called this impulse "salvage ethnography—the capturing of an authentic culture thought to be rapidly and inevitably disappearing." Importantly, salvage workers like Pratt must confront a contradiction. He has to believe "in both disappearing culture and the existence of informants knowledgeable enough about that culture to convey worthwhile information" (Deloria 1998, 90). Pratt faces another paradox: he is working to stamp out the tribal cultures he also wants to preserve. As was the case with many writers and politicians before him, a trope of the Indian fills this gap in logic. As Vizenor (1994, 11) argues, "Dominance is sustained by the simulation that has superseded the real tribal names." Pratt conceives of the Indian as a student to meet the burden of maintaining American national innocence. His fantasy of benevolence requires Indians to be figured as culturally childlike. Education supersedes alternative policies such as upholding treaties, segregating and confining Indians on reservations, or subduing Indians through war.

Through education, Pratt was convinced that the Indian could become the same as, or similar to, the white man. For the federal government, this particular trope of the Indian student justified not only the breaking of treaties in the Southern Plains but also ongoing westward expansion and land theft. Long viewed as a solution to the "Indian Problem," reservations now came under attack as segregated spaces keeping Indians from reaching the full potential of American citizenship. Pratt's reframing of Indian as student made way for the off-reservation boarding school system, which in turn amplified and spread allotment policies that reproduced private land ownership, nuclear family kinship structures, and English-language dominance. Pratt's myth of the Fort Marion prisoners, that he could transform fierce Indian savages into receptive students, laid the groundwork for the assimilation and allotment project that would drive Indian policy for the next century.

Figure 1.1. Plains Indian prisoners arriving at Fort Marion, Florida, ca. 1875. Photographer unknown. Courtesy, Beinecke Rare Book and Manuscript Library, Yale University, New Haven, CT.

We can see this shift from savage to student entering the public imagination through Pratt's famous before-and-after photographs. As Hayes Peter Mauro (2011, 2) has argued, the logic of assimilation "could be visually established for a broad public by means of photography and illustration." The before-and-after images of Carlisle students are some of the best-known artifacts from this archive. Many who do not know much about off-reservation boarding schools have seen the images of Native children in tribal dress and long hair beside their images in Victorian attire. Amelia Katanski (2005, 44) has shown that "to make it appear that the schools did succeed in their mission of cultural genocide, Pratt and his cohorts needed to control representations of their students, by sanctioning or producing only representations of total transformation." Pratt began this practice of documenting the transformation from savage to student with his prisoners at Fort Marion. In fact, one of the first things Pratt did upon arriving was have a "before" photograph taken of every prisoner. Three years later, Pratt had a stereograph taken of the same men clothed in the uniforms of the US military. This stereograph[4] was likely sold as a tourist item and is titled "A Picture of the Indian cut throats and scalpers who were confined in the

For a vivid description of ST. AUGUSTINE, READ BLOOMFIELD'S HISTORICAL GUIDE.

FLORIDA, THE LAND OF FLOWERS AND TROPICAL SCENERY.

Figure 1.2. Stereograph of Fort Marion prisoners in US military attire, ca. 1878. Courtesy, New York Public Library, New York City.

old Spanish fort as prisoners of war by the United States Government."[5] The before-and-after images became a visual shorthand for Pratt's larger project: enacting the complete transformation of Indian savages into citizens of the United States.

Pratt also viewed exemplary prisoners as evidence of his success in transforming savages to students and ultimately citizens. Etahdleuh Doanmoe was a young Kiowa man who later became a teacher at Carlisle. Pratt took a special interest in Doanmoe, calling him his "prize Florida boy" and insisting "he is born a blank like the rest of us" (Lookingbill 2007, 41). Doanmoe's sketchbook is the central document I study in this chapter. When Pratt curated and edited the sketchbook to give to his son, Mason, he pasted the "before" photograph of the Fort Marion prisoners inside the back cover and an "after" photograph inside the front cover. The "after" photograph shows five former prisoners including Doanmoe wearing US military uniforms. It was likely taken years after the men's incarceration once some prisoners came to work at Carlisle (Earenfight 2007b, 77). The photographic and textual narrative Pratt assembles in what he calls *A Kiowa's Odyssey* shows how he viewed Doanmoe as a test case for his Lockean theory of Indigenous identity. He believed indigeneity was a learned trait that could be reversed through education. He used the language of conversion to explain his views to a Baptist convention in 1883: "In Indian civilization, I am a Baptist because I believe in immersing the Indians in our civilization and when we get them under

Figure 1.3. Etahdleuh Doanmoe, ca. 1880. Courtesy, Archives and Special Collections, Dickinson College, Carlisle, PA.

holding them there until they are thoroughly soaked" (Utley 1964, xv). Figuring Indians as blank slates, or religious converts, ran parallel with Pratt's broader rhetorical project: to prove to the public that the Indian could be re-formed as a student of US culture, thereby rendering his tribal identity moot and solving the Indian Problem once and for all.

Pratt's theory was grounded in two established Euro-American colonial projects: Christian missionary education and government-sponsored civilization programs first envisioned by George Washington's secretary of war, Henry Knox, in 1789. Knox hoped to eventually subsume all tribal identities beneath the purview of American citizenship and planned a fifty-year window for Indians east of the Mississippi to integrate into Euro-American society. By extinguishing titles, denationalizing tribes, and leaving only "individual Indian landholders scattered as farmer-citizens among the whites," Knox believed the question of relations between whites and Indians would be resolved (McLoughlin 1981, 4). The civilization program reflected a federal policy based in cultural rather than racial differences between Euro-Americans and Indians. Indians were seen as uncivilized simply because they had not been adequately exposed to Euro-American cultural practices. To demonstrate their civilization, they would need to "dress, think, act, speak, work, and worship the way that rural United States citizens, ideally, did" (Purdue and Green 2005, 11). This policy fell apart in the face of Cherokee, Choctaw, Chickasaw, Seminole, and Creek resilience following settler encroachment into Indian Territory, leading the federal government to turn to forced removal policies in the 1830s. Nearly 100 years later, the federal government showed renewed interest in civilization programs after the violent campaigns on the Southern Plains fell out of public favor.

Pratt saw Doanmoe as a shining example of his vision for the Indian student paradigm. Doanmoe learned English and went on speaking tours in New York and New England to talk about his experience at Fort Marion. When his incarceration ended, Doanmoe decided to continue his education at the Hampton Institute and then recruited Kiowa and Comanche students for Carlisle, where he worked as a teacher during the years 1880–1882. But Doanmoe's story is much more complex than that of an unquestioning convert to Euro-American lifeways. In fact, the sketchbook he kept during his captivity crafts a powerful counter-narrative to Pratt's simplistic conversion theory. In the following section, I read Doanmoe's sketchbook as an example of the rhetoric of relations. This reading illuminates how the syncretic media of Plains pictography in Euro-American ledger books allowed Doanmoe to both envision and enact a de-colonial future for the Kiowa prisoners and their nation.

ETAHDLEUH DOANMOE'S SKETCHBOOK AND KIOWA FUTURITY

When Pratt arrived at Fort Marion with seventy-two prisoners, he gave them sketchbooks and colored pencils to occupy their time and encourage them to be industrious (i.e., make money by selling their drawings). As Angela Haas (2015, 191–192) has argued, it is difficult in colonial worldviews to see Indigenous peoples using the technologies of their moment. Pratt's limited sense of Plains textual traditions prevented him from understanding the subversive and strategic ways his prisoners used the sketchbooks and drawing pencils to continue to wage war against their captors. Pratt did not imagine that the sketches could be used to plot an escape or to chronicle prisoners' maintenance of their warrior identities through suicide and other acts of self-sacrifice. The prisoners' pictographic writing in the sketchbooks functioned as an interpretive and historical text through which they came to understand new relations to place and peoplehood. The sketches draw on Plains media such as winter counts, which record and preserve collective memory, so we can also read the sketches as manifestations of the prisoners' hopes that their sketches would return to the Southern Plains to enter into their nations' communal histories.

The Fort Marion sketchbooks exemplify how media operate through productive misunderstanding when two distinct cultural groups interact. Richard White's notion of the "middle ground" helps explain the intercultural accommodation and meaning making that occurred at Fort Marion. As White (1991, x) explains:

> On the middle ground, diverse peoples adjust their differences through what amounts to a process of creative, and often expedient, misunderstandings. People try to persuade others who are different from themselves by appealing to what they perceive to be the values and practices of those others. They often misinterpret and distort both the values and the practices of those they deal with, but from these misunderstandings arise new meanings and through them new practices—the shared meanings and practices of the middle ground.

To Pratt, the sketchbooks are Euro-American cultural tools used by children or students for educational and artistic purposes. Because he wants the prisoners to sell their products, the sketchbooks also become a way for them to learn about commerce and self-sufficiency. The sketchbooks fit within Pratt's civilization program and his rhetorical project to transition savages to students. For the prisoners, on the other hand, the sketchbooks parallel the ledger books they took from US soldiers in the Southern Plains as war trophies and then incorporated into their traditional practices of hide drawing (Berlo 2007a, 172). In this framework, the sketchbooks are historical tools, a means of building cultural memory in a new context of violence and coercion. For both groups, then, the sketchbook becomes a medium for negotiating meaning and fighting for cultural dominance. Yet on the middle ground, this medium accrues new functions beyond both groups' existing purposes and understandings. This space of negotiation and misunderstanding creates the fertile ground on which new relational rhetorics can emerge.

The sketchbook drawings are just one way Pratt and his prisoners negotiated power through their means of communication. Pratt spoke primarily through a Comanche interpreter, which indicates an ongoing translation process that chipped away at the authority and primacy of the English language at the prison (Lookingbill 2007, 38). Prisoners mixed Plains Sign Talk with English words to communicate across tribes,

indicating that they did not see English as a replacement for their existing languages but rather as a new tool to incorporate into processes of
intercultural meaning making (Lookingbill 2007, 45). When Kiowa prisoners planned an escape, they did so by mapping the territory around
Fort Marion in the very sketches Pratt so enthusiastically encouraged
them to draw. And when their plot was discovered, Pratt deployed his
(mis)understanding of Kiowa medicine to convince the prisoners of
his total control over their bodies and words. As Laura Mielke (Bellin
and Mielke 2011, 4) has noted, the colonization of North America
represents "a centuries-long process whereby the public actions of
Indians—individual, familial, communal, ceremonial, theatrical, political, literary—have countered, informed, and shaped the public actions
of European colonizers." At Fort Marion, Pratt and his supervisors in the
Department of War and the Indian Bureau had to shift their sense of
US cultural supremacy as different rhetorics accrued authority. To move
beyond the overly simplistic notion that Pratt forced the assimilation
of the prisoners and, later, Carlisle students, we need a framework that
privileges negotiation, accommodation, and mutual misunderstanding
in colonial encounters. Relations among prisoners, captors, Southern
Plains nations, and the United States shifted as a result of the rhetorical
tactics deployed by Indigenous rhetors imprisoned at the fort.

Pratt preserved Doanmoe's sketchbook and handed it down to
his son. Pratt intended for the sketchbook to provide evidence of
Doanmoe's complete conversion from savage to student. He captioned
the sketches with his own narrative and determined that the book
should be read from left to right, as in Western alphabetic reading conventions, rather than right to left, the Kiowa convention that Doanmoe
likely intended (Rasmussen 2014, 262). In recent years, these sketches
have gained increased scholarly attention thanks to the work of Phillip
Earenfight, who reassembled and reprinted the sketchbook in 2007.

While scholars have long viewed the sketchbook as an important
work of Kiowa art, my interest is in the text's rhetorical rather than
aesthetic properties. I read the sketchbook as a medium through which
Doanmoe made sense of his changing relations to land, peoplehood,
and language. Doanmoe engaged in two key practices: *strategic incorporation* of Euro-American conventions and *subterfuge* to maintain his Kiowa
identity while undermining the efforts of his captors. Doanmoe's sketchbook participates in what Mielke (Bellin and Mielke 2011, 5) has called
"tactical, often defiant enactments of Indianness" as he used Southern
Plains textual modes to both engage in and record resistance. Precisely
because settler audiences viewed Plains pictographs as culturally exotic

and authentically Indian, prisoners including Doanmoe were encouraged to draw in sketchbooks and sell their "art" to tourists. The notion of authentic Indianness and myths of the disappearance of Indian cultures in the West led Pratt and his contemporaries to preserve the drawings for posterity, and now they can be found in archives across what is currently the United States. Doanmoe's use of the rhetoric of relations is an important precursor to the strategies deployed by students at the Carlisle school. His rhetorical tactics enrich our understandings of the many media in which Native rhetors maintain their cultural identities in the face of settler-colonial violence.

Prior to post-bellum incursions by the US government, the Kiowa Nation's land base covered the prairies near the Yellowstone River and the headwaters of the Missouri River in the northern Great Plains. In the early nineteenth century, the Kiowa experienced a period of great prosperity and their number grew to 1,300, but a smallpox outbreak in 1825 devastated the tribe. The maxim "Behold, I stand in good relation to all things" is foundational to the Kiowa worldview. As disease and settler incursions threw traditional relations out of balance, the Kiowa went to war. Doanmoe joined in the insurgency against settler occupation with Comanche, Cheyenne, and Arapaho warriors and would eventually surrender to Colonel Pratt on February 23, 1875. The mass slaughter of buffalo by federal troops made these tribes' traditional subsistence practices impossible to sustain, which ultimately led to the Buffalo War of 1874 and the men's captivity during the period 1875–1878 (Lookingbill 2007, 31–35).

Etahdleuh Doanmoe's name means "Boy Hunting." He earned this honorific after his first buffalo kill at age fifteen (Rasmussen 2014, 259). As his name indicates, Doanmoe's identity centered around being a hunter. After the apocalyptic events of the Plains Wars and the near extinction of the buffalo, Doanmoe's rhetorical project would be to reclaim his "good relation to all things." Andrea Riley-Mukavetz and Malea Powell (2015, 144) have discussed how Indigenous rhetorics are grounded in good relations: "Relationships are material and we must work (with) them every day . . . a way into making something . . . is by understanding and examining one's relationship to the world, that it's a point of deeply complex inquiry." When Doanmoe cataloged his journey to Fort Marion in the sketchbook, it was a way into examining his new relations with land, language, and peoplehood. The sketchbook integrates his hunter and warrior identities with his new life as a prisoner. Alongside drawings of Captain Pratt's home and the fort's schoolroom, for example, Doanmoe included a sketch of two warriors killing buffalo.

He also recorded a shark hunting victory and captured the events of the allied tribes' surrender at Fort Sill. The sketchbook was a means to bridge his tribal and captive identities through pictographic representation of his shifting environment, role, and relations.

Kiowa pictography is a historical, textual, and mnemonic practice. As Janet Berlo (2007a, 172) writes, Kiowa men drew "images of their exploits, first on buffalo robes, and later on the pages of ledger books they took as war trophies or trade from whites." They also used pictographic calendars as communal historical texts: "A symbol for a key event of both winter and summer seasons of each year would be depicted, and tribal historians would use these documents as mnemonic devices to recall other important events as well" (172). Birgit Brander Rasmussen has argued that we should read these sketchbooks as communal pictographic calendars, or winter counts, as opposed to individual, biographical coup tales. According to Lakota historian Nick Estes (2019, 69), "Winter counts marked each year or winter by recording a significant event with a pictograph or hide (or sometimes on paper), accompanied by an oral recounting of the event." Rasmussen (2014, 270) argues that, like winter counts, the Fort Marion sketchbooks "represent a communal vision of collective identity formed around significant events." The captive warriors reproduced these traditional practices while also incorporating new techniques and imagery to understand and record their exile. Like his contemporaries, Doanmoe used colored pencils and drawing paper, media that had superseded traditional inks and hides following increased contact and trade with white settlers and merchants (Earenfight 2007b, 4). He incorporated new European techniques such as linear perspective as well (Lookingbill 2007, 44). Most significant, Doanmoe and the other captives created a new genre of imagery. They began to draw scenes of "courtship, feasting, and other aspects of domestic life" that did not traditionally appear in the pictographic record (Berlo 2007a, 172–174). These scenes illuminate how the Fort Marion prisoners used pictographic texts to remember and reinscribe ties to homeland, kin, and ritual. These men were writing new kinds of histories in a new environment. Doanmoe's sketchbook allowed him to make meaning of his violent and chaotic experiences while also maintaining ties to land, tribe, and history.

Domestic scenes were not the only innovations Etahdleuh Doanmoe and his fellow captives developed in their pictographic records. The prisoners used the sketchbooks to not only record but also wage acts of bravery and violent resistance. While Berlo (2007a, 174) has argued that Doanmoe's sketchbook avoided the topic of conflict between Indians and whites, this is only true in the sense that he did not depict battles on the Southern Plains. One of the most important and least discussed aspects of Doanmoe's strategy is his use of the sketchbook to both chronicle and wage acts of war against the US military. For the prisoners, the Indian Wars did not end with their captivity. They continued to resist as they traveled across the country and used their sketches to maintain continuity. They recorded acts of bravery in Plains textual traditions while innovating to address new circumstances and exigencies. Indeed, Brad Lookingbill (2007, 52) has described Doanmoe's sketchbook as the chronicle of "a warrior artist who 'counts his coup' in service to his people," and Rasmussen (2014, 271) has written that Doanmoe presents his journey as a "heroic act of engagement with the enemy for the benefit of the larger community." I read Doanmoe's sketchbook as a weapon of war and focus on his rhetorical practice as a continuation of the resistance he began as a warrior in his home territory. By reading the sketches in continuity with Plains practices such as coup tales and winter counts, I argue that Doanmoe draws to imagine a future for the Kiowa and other Plains nations in direct opposition to Pratt's attempts to extinguish Indigenous culture through education and assimilation. He draws on the particular affordances of the pictographic medium that only works in relation to oral performance. This means he can encode stories of rebellion and resistance that only a community fluent in Southern Plains pictographic writing can decode. The drawing is not the whole story.

Nearly a third of Doanmoe's sketchbook depicts the journey from Fort Sill to Fort Marion. This focus may have contributed to Pratt's title for the sketchbook, *A Kiowa's Odyssey*. Pratt clearly viewed the sketchbook as a heroic travel tale in the tradition of Homer and gave it a title to place it within a Western literary tradition. Pratt saw the sketchbook as a chronicle of the journey across the American landscape and as evidence of the cultural journey he believed Doanmoe undertook, from being an Indian to embracing Euro-American education and culture.

Eleven of thirty-one sketches focus on the journey by wagon, train, and steamboat that took place between April 28 and May 21, 1875. The prisoners were chained down and shackled in wagons as they traveled from Fort Sill to the Caddo station, where they got on a train. They traveled through Kansas City, Fort Leavenworth, St. Louis, Indianapolis, Louisville, Nashville, Chattanooga, Atlanta, Macon, and finally Jacksonville, where they boarded a steamboat to St. Augustine. Two Cheyenne chiefs, Lean Bear and Gray Beard, attempted escape and suicide during the journey, both of which feature in the sketchbook.

Doanmoe begins the sketchbook one year into his incarceration, which indicates that he focuses on those events that stood out as significant in retrospect rather than reporting on events as they occurred. This set of strategic decisions aligns with the Kiowa practice of pictography as historical record, an instance of the graphic impulse of Indigenous signification that "aspire[s] to be expressed in lasting formats" (Teuton 2010, xvii). The suicide and escape attempts of Lean Bear and Gray Beard appear implicitly and explicitly in sketches 13, 15, 16, and 17.

To read the sketchbook in the context of Indigenous cultures of print is to understand how the prisoners' sketches place embodied acts, oral storytelling, and written text *in relation* to document the events that took place on their cross-country voyage. As I discussed in the introduction, recent research on Native American media, cultures of print, and book history has thoroughly debunked earlier accounts by settler scholars that aim to place oral and literate communicative forms in opposition. Rather, we should view Indigenous communicative practices within the framework of a rhetoric of relations, where expressive traditions generate meaning at the interstices of different media: graphic, oral, alphabetic, and embodied. In Doanmoe's sketchbook, not only are word and image spun into a relational framework, but so, too, is embodied rhetoric. When a warrior comports himself with bravery and sacrifices his own life or body for the well-being of the group, this act is recorded in pictographic writing, which then functions mnemonically in the shared living memory of the tribe. This particular function of the Fort Marion sketches is crucial to understanding how Doanmoe inscribes and reproduces Indigenous resistance under his jailers' watchful eyes.

There is only one sketch in which Doanmoe draws an explicit scene of violence between US soldiers and Plains warriors ("The suicide was left in Nashville with a guard"). That sketch is a scene immediately following Lean Bear's wounding of two guards and attempted suicide near Nashville, Tennessee. Many other scenes depict the periphery of violent encounters on the Southern Plains, such as a narrowly avoided battle west of the Wichita Mountains when the US cavalry came across a Kiowa camp and the warriors distracted Pratt's men while the women and children returned to reservation land. There are also post-conflict scenes of surrender by the Kiowa warriors and peace talks between Kicking Bird and Pratt. But the closest Doanmoe comes to depicting an explicitly violent event is this sketch of Lean Bear under restraint by guards on the train platform in Nashville. As a prisoner of war drawing under the watchful eyes of his captors, Doanmoe would have wanted to avoid scenes depicting the violent events that transpired before, during, and after the

Figure 1.4. From Etahdleuh Doanmoe's sketchbook. Pratt captions the sketch "The suicide was left in Nashville with a guard, but recovered and was sent on to St. Augustine a few days later." Courtesy, Beinecke Rare Book and Manuscript Library, Yale University, New Haven, CT.

journey from Fort Sill to Fort Marion. This general avoidance of confrontational content makes the Nashville sketch particularly significant.

The scene shows the train at the station. The train faces the left, indicating its movement from the right to the left of the page. Tall buildings and small hills appear in the background. The second train car has dark ovals in each square window, which I read as the prisoners looking out toward the scene of action. The collective of prisoners acts as witnesses to Lean Bear's bravery. This speaks to the sketch's role in creating a communal historical record of the event. To the far left of the page, a crowd of onlookers encircles four soldiers who wear the blue uniforms of the US Army. Two are standing at attention with rifles and two are on the ground restraining Lean Bear, who wears bright red pants. His long hair reaches to the ground, and one leg kicks forward toward one of the soldiers. As Berlo (2007b, 154) explains, "In Plains ledger art, the action almost always moves from the right to the left of the page. Successful warriors and hunters, for example, are drawn on the right, facing left, toward their enemies and prey animals." In this sketch, the train moves from right to left, and Lean Bear faces left, implying that Lean Bear's courageous action is a victory if we consider that the events begin on the train (the right) and end on the platform (the left). Doanmoe draws Lean Bear as a successful warrior in the codes of Plains art.

We know from Pratt's memoir and his 1892 report to the Board of Indian Commissioners that Lean Bear used a pocketknife to wound two guards and stab himself eight times in the neck and breast (Glancy 2014, 104). This occurred 5 miles outside Nashville (Lookingbill 2007, 38). In sketch 15, Doanmoe shows the train arriving in Nashville. Pratt's caption reads "One of the Chiefs had attempted suicide on the cars just before." Out of thirty-one sketches, it matters that Doanmoe drew two of the Nashville arrival. While he did not explicitly draw the confrontation between Lean Bear and his captors on the train, he memorialized the event from a distant perspective, depicting the outside of the train as it pulled into the station. Like the pictographic writing of plains and woodland peoples, Doanmoe's pictography requires a cultural insider's memory and oral performance to make meaning. Pictographic writing in this case would have protected Doanmoe because the US soldiers would not have necessarily recognized this sketch as a record of Lean Bear's bravery. At the same time, Doanmoe captures the fight between Lean Bear and the soldiers and envisions a time when he can reconstruct and retain these events as part of the collective history of his nation. It is Pratt who narrativizes the sketch in alphabetic text and reframes a Kiowa pictographic history into a Euro-American alphabetic one. Far from avoiding the subject of violent engagements between prisoners and guards, then, the Nashville sketches memorialize Lean Bear's bravery and depict his suicide attempt as an honorable act of war.

The party left Lean Bear in Nashville with guards to treat his wounds until he was strong enough to travel. The guards then brought him to Saint Augustine several weeks later, but he refused to eat or speak during that time. On July 24, 1875, Lean Bear died of starvation (Glancy 2014, 26). As a Cheyenne chief, Lean Bear set an example of bravery, as he refused to surrender to incarceration by the US military. He attempted to die by his own hand, injuring his enemies in the process; when that attempt failed, he began a hunger strike to communicate his rejection of the US government's power over him. Lean Bear's rhetoric of refusal will be echoed by Ernest White Thunder, the son of a Lakota chief and one of Carlisle's first students.

Doanmoe, too, is taking part in Indigenous rhetorical practice by recording Lean Bear's story as a heroic victory. By using the conventions of Plains ledger art to place Lean Bear in the position of a victorious warrior/hunter, Doanmoe tells a very different story than Pratt's caption would imply. Pratt captions the sketch "The suicide was left in Nashville with a guard but recovered and was sent on to St. Augustine a few days later." Pratt dehumanizes Lean Bear by removing his name

Figure 1.5. From Etahdleuh Doanmoe's sketchbook. Pratt captions the sketch "The arrival in Nashville Tenn. One of the Chiefs has attempted suicide on the cars just before." Courtesy, Beinecke Rare Book and Manuscript Library, Yale University, New Haven, CT.

from the action, calling him "the suicide," a derogatory and shameful term in a Euro-American frame of reference. He does not understand that Lean Bear's sacrifice is a message to his fellow warriors. He does not understand Doanmoe's narrative of the event as an act of resistance as well. While Pratt editorializes Doanmoe's sketchbook with an alphabetic narrative of cultural and military superiority, Doanmoe's rhetoric of relations remains. In his own textual tradition, he depicts Lean Bear as a victorious warrior who will be remembered by those who witnessed his final acts against an overpowering oppositional force.

Just as Doanmoe captures Lean Bear's resistance in the Nashville sketches while avoiding explicit images of violence, he also memorializes the resistance of Cheyenne chief Gray Beard, who chose to die rather than enter into extended captivity at Fort Marion. Sketches 13 and 17 focus on Gray Beard's first and second suicide attempts, respectively. The first event took place at Fort Leavenworth, where Gray Beard hanged himself from the bars in his cell window. He was cut down by the Cheyenne elder Minimic (the prisoner who gave the petitionary prayer referenced at the start of this chapter). Gray Beard survived the first attempt to end his own life. Doanmoe draws a scene from the ten days the prisoners spent at Fort Leavenworth in sketch 13. Doanmoe shows a daytime view of the fort with the prisoners sitting outside on blankets. An American flag flies above the scene and barracks loom in the background, with visible bars on the windows. The prisoners would certainly not have read this sketch as serene, but Pratt's caption elides

Figure 1.6. From Etahdleuh Doanmoe's sketchbook. Pratt captions the sketch "The arrival in Jacksonville Florida." Courtesy, Beinecke Rare Book and Manuscript Library, Yale University, New Haven, CT.

Gray Beard's suicide attempt entirely: "The party remained at Fort Leavenworth two weeks and were taken out of the guard house daily for an airing" (Earenfight 2007b, 122). The flag, cannon, and barred windows all represent the violence of the US government toward Plains peoples, and Doanmoe's memorializing of the Fort Leavenworth part of their journey would certainly be narrated with a detailed recounting of Gray Beard's resistance to his captivity there.

Sketch 17 depicts the group's arrival in Jacksonville, Florida, on May 21, 1875. Once again, Gray Beard's heroic deeds are an invisible part of the story. Just before arriving in Jacksonville, he crawled out a window while the train moved at 25 miles an hour. The train backtracked, and guards searched for him. When he ran from some palmetto bushes, the guards shot him in the bowels. He died an hour later on the train (Glancy 2014, 105).

While others have viewed this as a failed escape attempt, I consider it a second attempt at suicide. One of the US soldiers, Hugh Lenox Scott, wrote that Gray Beard said he had wanted to die ever since being taken from home and put in chains (Berlo 2007b, 155).[6] Gray Beard must also have known the futility of escape. It would have been nearly impossible to make his way home from so far east. His death would serve as an example for his fellow prisoners of how they might continue resisting their captors and seeing themselves as warriors despite their displacement from their homelands. Gray Beard's actions did result in his death. He died just prior to arriving in Jacksonville, narrowly avoiding incarceration at the fort. Once again, Pratt's caption does not capture the context surrounding the sketch. He writes only "The arrival in Jacksonville Florida." From a Kiowa point of view, however, this sketch is not meant merely to be glanced over but instead to serve as a mnemonic device to recall the events of that day, the most important of which was certainly Gray Beard's deliberate and heroic decision to die rather than face indefinite captivity at the hands of his enemies. As in many of the sketches, Doanmoe takes a panoramic viewpoint and depicts the scene as a distant observer (Berlo 2007b, 155). This technique allows Doanmoe to avoid direct representation of the US soldiers' violence while also entering into the record a story of Gray Beard's death. He uses pictographic writing to create a document that, when read aloud in community, will recall an important act by a Cheyenne leader who kept his dignity and refused to accept defeat.

By depicting his journey across the continent and the brave acts of war waged by Gray Beard and Lean Bear, Etahdleuh Doanmoe envisioned the survival and continuance of Kiowa ways of life. These sketches are not merely curiosities, as Pratt views them. Given the mnemonic function of pictographic texts, these images only function within a communicative system indigenous to the Southern Plains, where a speaker will use the pictographs to recall and narrate key events. It is not necessary for Etahdleuh to depict the violent scenes between prisoners and soldiers because the pictographic text demands a living, speaking storyteller to function. For this reason, I argue that Etahdleuh was envisioning his texts reaching at least three audiences in different ways: his captors, his fellow prisoners, and his community back home. This third audience is the most important to understand the sketchbook as engaging a rhetoric of relations. The pictographs gesture toward a future time when Etahdleuh will be back with his kin, a time when he will want to record his experiences in the communal memory of his nation. Doanmoe's sketchbook is a text with a future. His sketches hold the hope of survival and resistance as conditions of colonization shift, as they inevitably will, to allow new means of reclaiming land and culture on the Southern Plains.

THE PRISONERS' BODIES AS SOVEREIGN MEDIA

As we have seen, sketches by Etahdleuh Doanmoe and the other prisoners were key sites of resistance against their captivity. These pictographic texts represent a rhetoric of relations that allowed the prisoners to maintain their tribal identities and covertly wage acts of war. The sketchbooks would also become a means for the Kiowa prisoners to plot an escape in April 1876. Lookingbill (2007, 44) has argued that the prisoners plotted their escape using drawings of military facilities, Anastasia Island, and the countryside around St. Augustine. Spring of 1876 was the same time frame when Doanmoe began drawing in his sketchbook. Doanmoe's sketchbook represents not only a means of preserving his experiences within the communal memory of his nation but also a strategic tool for ongoing campaigns against his captors.

Pratt describes the escape plot in great detail in his memoir, *Battlefield and Classroom* (1964). When he discovers what the Kiowa plan to do, he puts in place a ruse using Western medicine to make it appear he can disable, kill, and revive the prisoners at will. While the escape plot was a survival strategy employed by the Kiowas, a means to maintain their warrior identities within captivity, Pratt's response was a performance of colonial dominance. As the Kiowas forced their captors to continue to negotiate meaning within Indigenous frameworks of war, Pratt prevented future escape attempts through his manipulation of the concept of medicine in Plains cosmologies. This section looks at the use and rhetoric of medicine as a site of encounter at Fort Marion and the ways both Pratt and the prisoners themselves used the prisoners' bodies to negotiate power and control. The rhetoric of medicine became a rhetoric of relations in that dueling cultural conceptions of medicine changed the power relations between Pratt and the prisoners. In this case, the power to control meaning returned temporarily to Pratt.

Pratt (1964, 147) recounts that he became suspicious of the Kiowa prisoners when "their eyes were evasive" during daily inspections. Pratt's suspicion led him to coerce a Kiowa named Ah-ke-ah to reveal that the prisoners were plotting to leave the fort and travel west to their homeland (148). In Ah-ke-ah's account, the Kiowa prisoners would leave at the full moon (within three days) and had promised each other that they would not be re-captured alive. Under the leadership of White Horse and Lone Wolf, the men had made, collected, and hidden bows and arrows to kill game and protect themselves (148). Just as Cheyenne chiefs Gray Beard and Lean Bear had used their deaths to signify ongoing resistance to the US government, so, too, did the Kiowas plan to die as a rhetorical act to shore up the bravery of their peers. A year into their captivity, these men refused to be the reformed savages Pratt reported to his superiors. They did not fit the Indian-as-student myth Pratt was working hard to turn into national policy. The Kiowa prisoners continued to subvert Pratt's control by using the opportunity to sell bows and arrows to local tourists as a way to prepare an escape.

Pratt was developing a narrative that he possessed a unique ability to prevent future resistance from Indians, and an escape attempt was a massive setback. To regain his authority both at the prison and with the federal government, he needed to quickly and decisively reassert control over the prisoners' minds and bodies. To do so was a rhetorical project: he needed to demonstrate his cultural superiority and reframe the Kiowas as students, not warriors. Pratt's response was an elaborate performance of his power to know and act upon the prisoners' minds, bodies, and clandestine communications. Jessica Enoch (2002, 123) has noted that Pratt later fashioned himself the ever-present, all-knowing "Man-on-the-band-stand" at Carlisle, "his watchful gaze [having] much the same function as Foucault's Panopticon." In the context of the military prison at Fort Marion, Pratt solidified his control by communicating the scope of his surveillance. In Michel Foucault's (1979, 231) terms, he set about "maintaining them in perfect visibility, forming around them an apparatus of observation, registration, and recording, constituting on them a body of knowledge that is accumulated and centralized." At Fort Marion, the project of salvage ethnography mapped onto and amplified carceral logics of surveillance as a means to accumulate and centralize knowledge of the Indian.

When the escape plot comes to light, Pratt turns to violence to reassert dominance. After learning of the Kiowas' plan, he locks all the prisoners in the dining area, claiming that a bottle of poison has been stolen from the medical supplies. This gives Pratt an excuse to search each prisoner. During the search, a Comanche named Wyako threatens one of the men searching him; thus he becomes subject to the same punishment as the leaders of the escape plot. Lone Wolf is also searched and then confined by himself. During his search, White Horse says to the interpreter, "Tell the captain it is alright. I understand and I want him to kill me now" (Pratt 1964, 150). Pratt now has three prisoners to use as examples of his ultimate control. He contacts a commander across town, and they agree that the three prisoners will be held in dark-cell confinement off-site. Before sending the three men away, Pratt orchestrates "a little ceremony in connection with the transfer to impress all the Indians" (150). Pratt's use of the term *ceremony* here is telling. He draws on his experience of ceremony in Plains culture, as well as his own understanding of military ceremony, as a means of solidifying group cohesion and discipline. The escape plot becomes a moment "when cultural forms were up for grabs, when power was itself contested and shaped" (Deloria 2011, 316). Pratt hopes to manipulate the prisoners' understanding of his sovereign control of their bodies. He shapes meaning by incapacitating the bodies of the three prisoners, aware that this performance will resonate within conceptions of ceremony and medicine in Plains culture.

Pratt has soldiers march Wyako, Lone Wolf, and White Horse around the courtyard one at a time, late into the night, until each is exhausted, weak, and unable to stand. The other prisoners watch from their cells. As with the Kiowa escape attempt and the suicides of Lean Bear and Gray Beard, the audience for Pratt's performance is the other prisoners. The prisoners' bodies circulate rhetorically within the carceral environment. When each man is carried back inside, a doctor gives him a hypodermic needle injection to render him unconscious. Pratt writes that White Horse asked about the injection, and Pratt (1964, 151) responds to the interpreter, "tell him that I know the Indians have strong medicine and can do some wonderful things, but the white man has stronger medicine and can do more wonderful things, and I am having the doctor give him a dose of one of our strong medicines." Pratt explicitly engages Kiowa cosmology through his use of the term *medicine*. While he may not fully understand the significance of medicine in White Horse's culture, Pratt argues for his own cultural supremacy within an Indigenous cosmology. In her study of early American medical encounters, Kelly Wisecup (2013, 18) has argued that "intercultural texts were created as words, actions, and objects were appropriated from one context into others and as they were endowed with new meanings that were layered over previous significances." Much like the early colonists, Pratt uses his prisoners' bodies to communicate Euro-American dominance. But he also has a sense that medicine in Plains culture means something different than it does in his own. The overlap between Euro-American biomedical logics and Plains tribes' notion of sacred medicine creates a rhetorical relationality in which Pratt can push forward his strategy of control.

Medicine is a crucial component of Kiowa cosmology. In broad terms, Indigenous cultures conceptualize medicine as both physical and spiritual, and medicine is often synonymous with power (Wisecup 2013, 7–16). The Kiowa Sun Dance, for example, is initiated through the gathering of ten medicine bundles and their keepers. According to Benjamin R. Kracht (2017, 85), the Kiowa come into relationship with sacred power through a visionary experience where they learn the characteristics of their spirit benefactor and what objects such as "feathers, birds, animal parts, plants [and] minerals" should be "gathered and placed in a bundle wrapped in deer or buffalo skin." Songs and rituals work alongside this medicine bundle to bring about successful hunting and healing for the individual and the community (85). Medicine is a way of engaging with and benefiting from power, which for Plains tribes is "a sacred and transcendent force permeating the universe, present in everything" (58). When Pratt says that his medicine is stronger than

Indian medicine, he calls up this greater significance. Although Pratt himself may have a superficial understanding of Kiowa medicine, the term overlaps with his knowledge of Western medicine to render the prisoners unconscious. This rhetorical congruence is highly effective, and Pratt succeeds in suppressing further escape attempts as a result.

In his recounting of these events in *Battlefield and Classroom*, Pratt also attempts to control the narrative of his power over and benevolence toward the prisoners to the Euro-American audience of his memoir. He writes that just as the doctor is about to inject White Horse with the medicine, White Horse asks "will it make me good?" and Pratt says to the interpreter "tell him I hope so. That is the object" (1964, 151). This has always struck me as an unlikely way for White Horse to respond to a violation of his body, and I do not concede that he actually said this to Pratt. But what is interesting is how Pratt figures himself as a moral educator of a childlike Indian here. The medical scene in which Pratt enforces his violence and cruelty is cast as a clever way to educate Indians about Euro-American culture. When Pratt reports that White Horse wants the medicine to make him good, he is implying White Horse's consent, thereby maintaining the fantasy of benevolence that undergirds his entire project. This is Indian education by any means necessary. In retrospect, Pratt does not acknowledge the psychological cruelty of his acts. Rather, he writes himself as a dedicated teacher who will stop at nothing to make his unruly prisoners into good American students.

Once White Horse, Lone Wolf, and Wyako are unconscious, soldiers load the men into a cart in the courtyard to give the other prisoners the impression that they are dead. They remain in dark-cell confinement and shackles for four weeks off-site and then return for two more weeks of confinement under guard by their fellow captives. Pratt does not discuss how the other prisoners responded to his elaborate performance of medical dominance or how they reacted when the three, presumed dead, returned. Pratt (1964, 152) does report that his psychological torment of the prisoners allows him to convince White Horse, Lone Wolf, Wyako, and, by extension, the other men that they should "accept patiently all your punishment and await the outcome, and the Government will in its own time bring to pass whatever it thinks best."

Pratt successfully performed medical dominance because he generated new intercultural meanings of medicine that allowed him to communicate his power over the bodies of his prisoners. But Pratt was not the only one who used embodied rhetorics and the emergent intercultural concept of medicine to negotiate power. As captured in Doanmoe's sketchbook, Lean Bear and Gray Beard communicated resistance through their embodied acts. Other prisoners engaged in similar tactics. Big Moccasin, a Cheyenne prisoner, died of uremic poisoning on November 4, 1875, after tying a string around his penis so he could not urinate (Glancy 2014, 28). He used his body to communicate his resolve to never succumb to his captors' demands. His audience was the guards and the other prisoners. A year after the Kiowa escape attempt, when Pratt believed he had dismantled his prisoners' resistance, Cheyenne prisoner Howling Wolf entered his body into the ongoing negotiation of control as well. He stared into the sun, causing his vision to fail. According to the prison doctor, Howling Wolf had a "pterygium on the white of the eye extending to the cornea" (Glancy 2014, 81). In the summer of 1877, the US Department of War granted permission for Howling Wolf to go to the Massachusetts Eye and Ear Infirmary to treat his loss of vision. Dr. Henry Lyman Shaw found pterygia in both eyes and performed surgery, which partially restored Howling Wolf's sight (85). When doctors asked Howling Wolf how he had damaged his vision, he said "he had stared into the sun while seeking visions" (85). While these events are reported by doctors' letters in Euro-American biomedical terms, Howling Wolf's own language refers back to Cheyenne medicine and his attempt to perform the Sun Dance ritual in captivity.

On the Southern Plains, Sun Dance festivals took place in the late spring. Howling Wolf's condition developed in late spring of 1877 and was treated that summer, indicating that he participated in his nation's rituals of renewal. While Sun Dances varied among groups, the ceremony would generally last for weeks as different bands joined together to plan raids, bison hunts, and war expeditions while renewing their community through ritual, gift exchange, courtship, and marriage (Kracht 2017, 197). The Sun Dance ceremonies involved great personal sacrifice for the well-being of another or of the collective. Lakota writer Luther Standing Bear refers to the Sun Dance as a sacrificial ceremony. He describes men dancing for three or four days without food or water until fainting and men offering their bodies to be pieced by knives and suspended by the flesh (Standing Bear 2006a, 119–122). This ceremony of personal sacrifice for the well-being of the collective ties together much of the embodied resistance that occurred at Fort Marion. Perhaps Howling Wolf stared into the sun seeking visions that would have shown him a way forward from captivity and back to his nation. Perhaps he performed this act to disrupt the enculturation process to which he was subjected. Perhaps he sacrificed his sight for the well-being of his fellow captives and his nation and homeland. While we cannot know Howling Wolf's motivations beyond what he reported to his doctors, we can understand his embodied resistance within the context of the acts of the other Cheyenne and Kiowa prisoners around him. When Pratt demanded assimilation and obedience from the prisoners, they resisted with their bodies. These embodied rhetorics indicate the prisoners' continued engagement with their nations and warrior identities, as well as their personal sacrifices to shore up the courage and survival of their peers. Their rhetorics created relations between embodied and graphic forms of media to shift relations between Indigenous and settler groups.

At Fort Marion, prisoners and their captors engaged in an ongoing struggle for rhetorical dominance. What emerged was a middle ground where technologies such as sketchbooks and medical treatments accrued new meaning as each cultural group tried to understand the other. But this middle ground was not a space of shared power. The prison at Fort Marion was a site of almost total colonial dominance where Pratt tried to control the bodies and minds of the prisoners. For Pratt, the warriors' incarceration opened an opportunity to cement his own ideology into federal Indian policy. He worked in any media available, from photographs to memoir, to propagate a new myth of Indianness—the savage transformed into an obedient student who could one day assimilate fully into the mature state of American citizenship. At the same time, his prisoners refused to become disembodied parables for the justification of colonization. They used their bodies to make visible the violence of the US government. Through suicide, escape attempts, and self-mutilation, these prisoners sacrificed their bodies to shore up the collective. Through a Kiowa rhetoric of relations, Doanmoe captured the acts of these brave men and envisioned a future for their texts and their tribes on the Southern Plains.

2

PLAINS SIGN TALK
A Rhetoric for Intertribal Relations

Early in 1878, the US Department of War released the Fort Marion prisoners. Seventeen of the detainees decided to continue their education at the Hampton Normal and Agricultural Institute in Virginia. They arrived by steamer in April of that year. Former Union general Samuel Chapman Armstrong directed the Hampton Institute, which had operated since 1868 as a school for emancipated African Americans. Armstrong at first agreed to take only one Indian student. Richard Henry Pratt convinced him to take all seventeen for what he called the "experiment," but only if Pratt could secure private funding for the men's tuition, room, and board (Molin 1998, 84). The prisoners had been learning English during their detention, and the federal government considered the possibility of an Indian program at Hampton to be a promising path for their continued assimilation. Secretary of the Interior Carl Schurz and President Rutherford B. Hayes were particularly enthusiastic, with Hayes reporting to Congress that "the result of the experiment, if favorable, could be destined to become an important factor in the advancement of civilization among Indians" (quoted in Molin 1998, 86). In 1879, following the success of the Hampton program, the US Congress approved funding and provided the cavalry barracks in Carlisle, Pennsylvania, for the establishment of the first off-reservation boarding school.

After the Fort Marion detainees were established at Hampton, Pratt traveled to the Dakotas to secure more students. He returned on November 5, 1878, with forty boys and nine girls ages ten to twenty-five; most were Dakota youths from the Yankton Agency along with some Mandan, Arikara, and A'aninin (Gros Ventre) children. A Cheyenne student and former Fort Marion prisoner named Little Chief greeted the new arrivals "in the expressive sign-language, that all could understand" (Ludlow 1881, 662; see also Molin 1998, 86). This language, known as Plains Sign Talk (PST), developed in the multinational context of the Southern Plains and was used by the Pawnee, Shoshone, Cheyenne,

DOI: 10.7330/9781646420872.c002

Arapaho, Crow, and Siouxan tribes for diplomacy and trade (Yandell 2012, 536). PST became a powerful counter-literacy at Carlisle where teachers demanded that students give up their national languages for a single shared tongue—English. As a rhetoric of relations, this gestural language afforded students a means of intertribal communication that was illegible to their teachers. In fact, Carlisle teachers and Pratt himself *mis*read and underestimated the communicative importance of PST, viewing it as a form of disabled communication that students would leave behind as they learned English words. As this chapter weaves through logics of language, race, and disability in the late nineteenth century, students' use of Plains Sign Talk serves as a grounding case study in how Indigenous languages were interpreted by educational reformers. In an extraordinary feat of un-seeing Indigenous literacies, Pratt would base his English-only curriculum on the assumption that Indians and the deaf would benefit from an identical, gesture-based approach to literacy education. This interpretation of PST had far-reaching effects for early pedagogy and curriculum at Carlisle. But as in all of the cases I discuss, Plains Sign Talk took on new importance in the context of the multilingual, multinational boarding school environment. The language became a rhetorical mode that facilitated intertribal relations and ongoing opportunities for resistance both in and beyond the school itself.

FROM MISSIONARY TO GOVERNMENT-SPONSORED INDIAN EDUCATION

Pratt's educational work at Fort Marion and Hampton was the first step in a paradigm shift in Indian education from missionary-run bilingual education in Indian Country to government-run English-only boarding schools. During the Assimilationist Era, this shift in Indian education tracked a parallel shift in land policy. Beth Piatote maps the assimilation period onto the years between 1879 (the opening of the Carlisle school) and 1934 (the passage of the Indian Reorganization Act). Piatote (2013, 1) writes, "These events inaugurated and suspended the two most dominant policies of the era: the forced removal of Indigenous children from their families to attend government-funded boarding and day schools and the allotment of reservation land into severalty." Indian education facilitated land policies that aimed to free up as much territory as possible in the American West for settlement. If students no longer spoke their tribal languages or passed on their cultural heritage, reformers believed surrendering their national identities and lands would naturally follow.

This paradigm shift shows up in curricular and pedagogical texts from the Carlisle archive. In turn, these curricular materials demonstrate how shifting racialized beliefs about Native Americans directly impacted the pedagogy teachers and administrators implemented. This chapter looks at why and how Carlisle educators rejected all existing literacy texts for Native students in their own languages in favor of a gestural curriculum for Indigenous language eradication. The pedagogical and curricular writings of Carlisle's first educators demonstrate their belief that Indigenous languages were holding students back from learning how to be American citizens. By examining these materials and practices for their intersection with theories of embodiment and disability, it becomes clear that assimilationist literacy education is rooted in nineteenth-century beliefs about embodied difference and national belonging.

In the model of missionary education that preexisted Carlisle, bilingualism or multilingualism was not seen as a problem so long as religious conversion and biblical literacy were the goals of language and literacy education. Christianizing Indians had been a concern of Euro-American settlers since the early 1600s with Puritan John Eliot's first proselytizing efforts with the Massachusett Nation. After the founding of the American Board of Commissioners for Foreign Missions (ABCFM) in 1810, Protestant missionaries played a key role in printing and teaching the Bible, from the Cherokee Nation to the Kingdom of Hawaii.[1] Missionary-sponsored Indian education was formalized as a national interest in 1819 when the US Congress established a "civilization fund" that went primarily to missionary societies (Spack 2002, 4). Ruth Spack writes that in day schools and missionary boarding schools, "classes were typically conducted in vernacular to promote understanding of biblical teachings, although most mission schools eventually added English-language instruction" (4). The long history of missionary education resulted in countless primers and other teaching materials in Indigenous languages as well as many experienced teachers who spoke those languages.

In the same period, missionaries took an interest in deaf education. Congregational minister Thomas H. Gallaudet opened the first American school for the Deaf in Connecticut in 1817. Douglas C. Baynton has argued that Protestant missionaries saw an overlap in Indian and deaf education because they romanticized the two groups as pre-literate. Based on their belief that God had created oral language and gesture before humans adopted writing, missionaries considered so-called primitive languages and gesture to be closer to the divine because they preexisted the fall of man (Baynton 1996, 37). This belief in the purity of pre-alphabetic forms allowed multiple literacies to thrive in educational environments. As Darwinian evolution grew in prominence, however, reformers in both the Indian and Deaf Education movements wanted to unite the nation under a standardized English literacy. They believed European speech and writing were ultimately the most evolved forms of human expression. Tribal languages and deaf sign languages became indicative of barbarism and savagery, with "Darwin himself [writing] of gestures as a form of communication 'used by the deaf and dumb and by savages'" (Baynton 1996, 42). If these literacies were allowed to persist, Darwinian thought proposed that they could reverse evolution and delay national progress. Pratt shared the beliefs of his contemporaries that English was the language of individualists and that by learning English, Indian students could better acculturate into Euro-American society (Spack 2002, 29).

As social-evolutionist thought gained prominence, Pratt built a literacy program in explicit opposition to earlier missionary efforts. Pratt propagated his social evolutionist views in Carlisle periodicals and in speaking tours across the United States. He often had Carlisle students parrot his views in their own writing, such as this opinion piece by Samuel Townsend (1881b, 2) the Pawnee student editor of the *School News*:

> The English language is much better than any Indian language. Some missionaries have spent much time in making books in the Indian language. There are a great many words in English that the Indians have no word for so the white people who make the Indian books have to make new Indian words. So the Indians have to learn the new Indian word. Now we don't know much about it, but we believe the Indians can all learn to speak the same as the whites.

Here, we can see that Pratt is teaching students that the English language is more developed, efficient, and specific than Indigenous languages. Townsend writes that tribal languages lack sufficient vocabulary to be accurately translated into writing. Even more important, the labor of translating English to a Native language is inefficient and burdensome to white educators. To be included in the US nation, students would have to use a language that shared the imagined superior characteristics of Euro-American culture—efficiency and intellectual advancement.

Pratt's view that tribal languages were underdeveloped led him to disqualify all preexisting teaching materials and all experienced multilingual missionary teachers. He now had to design an Indian education policy from scratch. It was certainly lost on Pratt that the far more expedient method for English education would be to engage existing

Figure 2.1. A classroom with male students at the Carlisle Indian School, ca. 1880. Photo by John N. Choate. Notice pictographic sketches of horses on the chalk board. Courtesy, Cumberland County Historical Society, Carlisle, PA.

bilingual texts to teach students to speak in both English and their Native tongues. Only the twisted colonial logic of destroying to replace makes the Native language seem inefficient in this scenario. Pratt thought he could prevent students from speaking their home languages by replacing those languages with signs. His educational philosophy is an eerie mirror of the settler colonial project wherein the settler state destroys Indigenous nations to replace them with the settler language and a settler citizenry (Wolfe 2006, 388).

Pratt was not alone in his view that a program for English-only education was in the national interest. For the US government, Indigenous nations represented a troubling irregularity in US sovereignty and had since the nation's founding. When Indian Wars broke out in the Southern Plains after the Civil War, there was a public outcry for a less violent approach to settlement of the West. As a result, the late 1860s saw a shift in colonial strategy to the "Peace Policy," which argued that "it costs less to civilize than to kill" (Spack 2002, 17). The English language was the linchpin of the Peace Policy. Commissioner of Indian Affairs Nathaniel Taylor argued that English could erase differences between Euro-American and Indigenous peoples, creating "one homogenous mass" that could be more easily controlled by the government (quoted in Spack 2002, 17). The notion that English could unite diverse and opposing groups led to policies based on the belief that a standardized English could create national cohesion. Taylor's beliefs echo those of many reformers known as the Friends of the Indian but also resonate with emerging thought in the Deaf Education Movement. When reformers from both the Indian and deaf education efforts noticed that Native Americans were using sign language to assist in intertribal communication and the Deaf were using sign language to communicate with other Deaf people, this commonality rebounded negatively on each group.

As English became the accepted standard for national belonging, sign languages began to be seen as evidence that Deaf and Native Americans were culturally, linguistically, and cognitively behind the Euro-American citizen ideal. This paradigm led educational reformers to attempt to eradicate all communicative forms they viewed as non-standard Englishes, including Indigenous spoken languages and deaf sign languages. K. Tsianina Lomawaima and Teresa L. McCarty (2006, 5) have argued that "standardization has segregated and marginalized Native peoples and others as it has circumscribed a narrow zone of tolerable cultural difference." By looking at the role of Plains Sign Talk at Carlisle, I explore how educational reformers understood different forms of languaging and how Carlisle students manipulated those understandings to create culturally sustaining opportunities. There are so many ways this nineteenth-century paradigm of enforced monolingualism persists in today's writing classrooms, particularly in the fantasy of benevolence within which Pratt and his contemporaries operated. By returning to pedagogical and curricular materials from the early efforts to standardize English education, scholars and teachers of writing must attend to how cultural beliefs about literacy become a tool of colonization. The archive of the Carlisle school's early curriculum demonstrates how important it is for writing teachers to act as vigilant defenders of non-standard Englishes in their classes as they convene in the legacy of these colonial roots.

A NOVEL CURRICULUM FOR INDIANS

With no model to follow, Carlisle's curriculum began as a trial-and-error endeavor. Within a few months, Pratt turned to the Deaf Education Movement for guidance. He wrote about how he developed his new curriculum in the first edition of the Carlisle publicity newspaper, the *Eadle Keatah Toh*:

> Professor Keep and Dr. Porter, well known educators of the deaf and dumb, during a recent visit here, were struck by the many features held in common by the Indians and the deaf and dumb in their sign languages. The teachers received a number of valuable hints from the learned gentlemen with reference to the way of teaching the dusky pupils of English. (Pratt 1880b, 3)

When Pratt, John Robinson Keep, and Samuel Porter collectively witnessed Plains Sign Talk, they decided that it was similar to deaf sign language. But Pratt had been familiar with PST for many years and had not previously viewed the language in this way. He had encouraged the use of PST at Hampton when new students arrived from the West. At Fort Marion, he had employed an interpreter fluent in both Cheyenne and PST and had one of his prisoners give a talk in "Indian sign language" during a performance to raise money for the prisoners' education (Pratt 1964, 163–188). Although Pratt was not fluent in PST, he did have to engage with this language as he lived and communicated with the prisoners at Fort Marion and Hampton. He clearly viewed the language as an effective way to communicate across linguistic barriers and an important intercultural tool. Yet in 1880, Keep and Porter's visit caused Pratt to reinterpret his understanding of PST. Due in part to changing theories of deaf education in the post-bellum period, Keep and Porter collapsed deaf sign language and Plains Sign Talk so that Pratt could enforce an English-only policy.

When Porter and Keep visited Carlisle, they made recommendations based on a historically specific set of logics around race, embodiment, and disability. They ascribed cultural deficiency to Native students because of the racialized ways they read students' embodied language practices. Amelia Katanski has studied how educational reformers in the late nineteenth century, particularly the "Friends of the Indian" involved in the boarding school movement, espoused the theory of social evolutionism. They imagined "a linear, hierarchical relationship among races. The ideology was accompanied by a 'replacement' model of identity, which claimed that education would totally transform student[s] as they 'progressed' from tribal 'savagery' to Western 'civilization'" (Katanski 2005, 4). Once again, the settler-colonial logics of elimination through "replacement" emerge in language education (Wolfe 2006, 387). Because reformers believed English could transform Indians into American citizens, vestiges of tribal languages constituted a direct threat to the advancement of any "civilizational" program. Hence, pedagogies grounded in social evolutionism encouraged an extreme standardization of English structure and usage.

On this issue of standardization as an educational and national value, Porter wrote to Pratt:

> There is a point upon which I should think there would be need of very determined effort on the part of the instructors. I refer to the tendency to employ broken English. I think that may prove one of the greatest difficulties you will have to contend with. With this also, and of course the

tendency to use Indian idioms and Indian order of words, the only way
must be not even to allow, except in extreme cases, any such violation of
correct usage to go uncorrected. (Porter 1880a, 4)

Porter insists that all tribal language features must be extinguished for
students to learn English. His word choice emphasizes Native language
as a problem or a pathology to be rooted out. Porter fears "broken
English," which he characterizes as the English instructor's "greatest
difficulty." The notion of broken English makes language a material
problem, like a broken bone—non-standard English is a sign that the
body is not operating properly in the logics of the Euro-American national project. Porter's word choice of "extreme cases" also indicates
that he is viewing language variation as an embodied problem, like an
extreme case of a disease. He seems to suggest that deviance from standard English, whether in idiom or word order, could further disable the
students and keep them from achieving the imagined linguistic purity
that would demonstrate the success of the social evolution project. To
reframe Porter's point in the language of "replacement," we might say
that just as settler society must replace Indigenous society on the land,
so, too, must English replace all Indigenous languages. There can be
no remnant of Indigenous nations left to challenge the settler society's
claim to the land; there can be no remnant of Indigenous language features in the students' English either.

Porter associates "broken English" with a racialized Indian body that
is culturally dysfunctional. Later in his career, Pratt would articulate his
understanding of Indigenous cultures as disabled as well. In 1892, he
gave a speech at the Conference of Charities and Correction arguing
against on-reservation education in which Indians "formulate the notion
that the government owes them a living and vast sums of money; and by
improving their education on these lines, but giving no other experience
and leading to no aspirations beyond the tribe, [we] leave . . . them in
their chronic condition of helplessness, so far as reaching the ability to
compete with the white race is concerned. It is like attempting to make
a man well by always telling him he is sick" (Pratt 1973, 265). Porter
used the language of disability to describe the Carlisle students' non-
standard English, and Pratt applies similar language here to describe
on-reservation education. He refers to the "chronic condition" of helplessness and suggests it is impossible to "make a man well by always telling him he is sick." Here, Pratt blames Indigenous peoples themselves
for their dependence on government annuities, failing to recognize that
those annuities were stipulated in treaties when these nations ceded or
were forced to leave their ancestral lands. Instead, Pratt believes there

is something inherent in Indigenous cultures that leads to these "sick" notions of helplessness and dependence. Only by taking children away from their culture and kin can this sickness be cured. As such, English-only education at boarding school becomes the solution to the imagined disability of Indigenous languages but also promises to end the reservation system forever, creating a single language, culture, and land base for the settler society.

Given the overlap in Pratt's and Porter's beliefs about Indigenous languages and cultures, it is not surprising that deaf educators greatly influenced Pratt's development as an Indian educator. In August 1880, about six months after Keep and Porter's visit, Pratt (1880a, 2) reported to the Congressional Indian Committee that teachers were using Keep's *First Lessons for the Deaf and Dumb* (1875). This instructional method illuminates the day-to-day procedures that enacted discourses of Native disability with material results for Native students' learning. In Keep's curriculum, students first learn nouns and names by associating physical objects with words. One sample lesson from Keep's textbook asks a teacher to hold up a sponge, write the word *sponge* on a slate, and then ensure that the correspondence between word and object is clear to the students. They reproduce the word on their own slates or spell it aloud. The relationship between signifier and referent here is primarily alphabetic, which makes sense in a classroom of deaf students who would not hear a word spoken orally. It does not make sense, however, for a class of Native students who can certainly access language in its spoken form. The "word method," as Pratt calls is, circumvents oral language entirely, stripping students of their communication and, paradoxically, disabling their means of communication. This is an educational example of how, as Siobhan Senier and Clare Barker (2013, 125) have noted, "settler colonialism is implicated in the production of Indigenous disability, discursively and materially." This pedagogy constructs Native students as people with no concept of the relationship between words and things. It privileges the alphabetic at the expense of the oral. Students are asked to spell the word aloud so the oral is subsumed beneath the logic of the written. Pratt embraces Keep's method because he believes it will allow him to block students from speaking in their Native languages and more quickly extinguish tribal oral literacies.

Another key effect of this curriculum is to center linguistic authority and the power of naming on the teacher. In the lesson on verbs, Keep suggests first that the teacher "draw the attention of all upon himself," centering his own linguistic authority. Then,

The teacher takes the sponge and throws it, writing immediately upon his own large slate, Mr. _____ threw a sponge. A sponge they know, and Mr. _____ they know. As they look at the sentence, some of the brighter members of the class will show that they understand what the new word means, by making the sign for throwing. (Keep 1875, 6)

In this example, oral language is again sidestepped, this time in favor of both gesture and alphabetic text. This lesson attempts to block Native students from associating a new word, "throw," with their existing term for the same action. Unlike bilingual pedagogies, Keep's text does not add to students' existing means of communication but attempts to block them from the act of translation. At the same time students are blocked from accessing their oral literacies, the Euro-American teacher is placing himself or herself at the center of meaning making.

This relationship between language and authority is mirrored in the object lesson, a method Pratt used alongside Keep's text. The object lesson was a popular nineteenth-century pedagogical method for infants and young children where an image represents an object that is accompanied by an explanatory text (Crain 2000, 119). Pratt used Janet Byrne's object-lesson book *Picture Teaching*, arguing that it was "especially adapted to Indian work" (1880a, 2). According to Patricia Crain (2000, 121), object lessons had "the effect of emphasizing the material objects while increasing the authority of the voice." While the object lesson was designed to center the authority of the mother in the white, middle-class home, at Carlisle that authority rested with the white teacher. She gained the power to order things in the world. In the context of Carlisle, the picture-teaching method reorients language relations to position Euro-American teachers at the center of language acquisition. The teacher replaces the parents and extended kinship networks Indigenous students drew upon in their home cultures. Lomawaima and McCarty (2006, 31) characterize Native American pedagogies as "language-rich contexts for education" where instruction was embedded in names, songs, and stories. They argue that "centuries of plain language, perplexing myths, lyrical songs, demanding questions, scolds and lectures, words of comfort and love and more—all have contributed to the language-rich life surrounding and nurturing Native people. Language has been a key, but not exclusive, medium of instruction in Indigenous educational systems" (36). At Carlisle, teachers replace the kinship networks that allowed Indigenous languages to pass from one generation to the next. This colonial strategy disrupts tribal continuance through literacy education.

Janet Byrne's object-lesson primers work in a very similar way to Keep's method: both circumvent oral communication *and* translation.

In Byrne's *Picture Teaching* (1869), students see alphabetic text alongside a picture of an object, such as an egg or an ax. These lessons prevent students from translating their existing words into new English words. They are not adding new language but replacing their existing words with English. In this way, English-only education achieves sweeping outcomes through day-to-day techniques of linguistic disruption. The racial assumptions at work in the settler society structure literacy lessons, which then create a feedback loop to replace Indigenous rhetorical sovereignty with settler language, literacy, and land rights.

Carlisle teachers established their power to name not only objects but students as well. Students' names were often the first victims of the Carlisle curriculum. As Brenda J. Child (1998, 29) explains, "Government teachers complained that the Indian names were unpronounceable, pagan, and sometimes even embarrassing." Students were stripped of their names for the same reason Pratt refused to use primers translated into Native languages—Euro-American educators did not want to engage in intercultural communication and translation. In his memoir *My People the Sioux*, Luther Standing Bear (2006b, 136) recalls his first class at Carlisle and the loss of his Lakota name:

> Our interpreter came into the room and said "Do you see all these marks on the blackboard? Well, each word is a white man's name. They are going to give each one of you one of these names by which you will hereafter be known." None of the names were read or explained to us, so of course we did not know the sound or meaning of any of them.

Students took on such peculiar titles as Rutherford B. Hayes and George Washington. In a sense, the first alphabetic literacy lesson ("these marks on the blackboard") required students to obscure their identities and kinship ties with new names. It is also striking that Standing Bear recalls a translator being with them in the room. Multilingual communication was always an available option and must have been used when students first arrived. But all communication had to be reoriented and contorted to fit the English-only orthodoxy at the center of the school's mission. This pedagogy discounted a multilingual alternative that would have done much to distribute authority between Euro-American and Indigenous epistemologies. To justify the departure from the established precedent of multilingual education, Pratt and his fellow educators had to view Native students as disabled by their language.

The rhetoric of disability was not the only sense in which literacy education at Carlisle was an embodied process. Pratt believed Indian students would best learn English by expressing the language with their bodies. In a report to the commissioner of Indian affairs in 1882, he had head teacher C. M. Semple explain the teaching methods:

> Almost from the first, by the use of slate and blackboard the pupils were taught to write and read the names of objects, or short sentences—using script—describing actions. "Harry ran." "Mattie ran." "Ina ran." written upon the board by the teacher, following the action by the child, copied upon the slate, at first almost illegibly, was one of the first lessons given a class of little Pueblos who came to us ignorant of English and without previous schooling . . . Running, jumping, ball throwing, paper throwing, drinking, eating etc. afforded amusement and exercise, alternating with the really difficult first lessons in writing. To expedite the process of learning to write, the sentences, or words, were written upon the board by the teacher, and after being almost erased, the little hands were guided in tracing the characters. This device, and a judicious amount of commendation and criticism secured success in the manual effort which in this method presents the only real difficulty. (Quoted in Report from Richard Henry Pratt 1882)

The report references Keep's textbook as the source of the curriculum two years after his initial visit, suggesting that this remained the primary approach for the entirety of the first students' three-year term at the school. To learn verbs, children had to enact the word with their bodies: running, jumping, ball throwing, and performing similar actions. It is as though the English language entered the bodies of the students to create a racial transformation. In this way, the students' bodies became conduits for the English language. Writing English was also an embodied process guided by the white educators—students traced sentences written by their teachers, and the teachers went so far as to physically guide their "little hands." The English-language–learning curriculum aimed to change the pupils' embodied movement. If language is a racialized trait in English-only logics and race is seen as residing in the body, a certain alchemy occured in this training process. Students were imagined to shed their culture as the English language entered and inoculated the Indigenous body, making it fit for entry into the Euro-American citizenry.

All of this is to say that both language and literacy development are embodied processes. Learning to write letters and to create sounds with the mouth and tongue are bodily acts through which children learn English. At Carlisle, teachers took on the role of parents as they forced their students' bodies and words into new shapes. Semple reports on how teachers manipulated the students' mouths to teach them proper annunciation: "It is often necessary to <u>show</u> the Indian pupil the proper position of the teeth, tongue, and lips and <u>insist</u> upon his imitation. When he finds that it is <u>possible</u> to make the difficult sounds, a great deal is done toward success in English speaking" (quoted in Report from Richard Henry Pratt 1882, original emphasis). I imagine teachers not only modeling their own tongue and lip positions but also touching the students' faces and moving their mouths into the shapes that create standardized English sounds. The emphasis on the words "show," "insist," and "possible" indicates a power dynamic in which the teacher imagines herself as the authority figure who must "insist" on her students' bodily conformity to make English "possible" for them. The body is the site of English-language development, and the racialized Indigenous body comes under the control of the Euro-American teacher. She holds the power to make her students' bodies and words fit within the settler society.

To study the rhetorical dimensions of literacy, according to John Duffy (2007, 3), is "to chart the symbolic environments in which reading and writing take place, and to look at how these environments influence the practice, dissemination, and meanings of literacy." During the Allotment Period, Indigenous languages and literacies accrued meaning within discourses of social evolutionism and attendant ideas about the racialized and disabled body. Pratt's literacy project was both assimilationist and eugenicist. The pedagogy through which he enacted that project aimed to eradicate Indigenous lifeways and nations in North America by destroying not only language but also the kinship lines through which language was passed down. Language assimilation has not been fully understood as an embodied process. Because Carlisle students' bodies were racialized through their languages, English-only training sought to move, shape, and alter them to destroy Indigenous identities and replace them with settler culture.

CONSTELLATING LITERACY, DISABILITY, AND RACE

When Carlisle students used Plains Sign Talk, they drew on a familiar and expedient language to communicate with each other in an unfamiliar environment. When Pratt, Keep, and Porter observed PST, they did not see savvy students drawing on their rhetorical repositories to engage the basic human need to communicate. Instead, they made sense of PST within late nineteenth-century theories about fixed racial characteristics that classified language users in a taxonomy of cultural development. To make sense of this constellation of racialization, disability, and language, we need to understand how intercultural rhetorics emerge and interact in a site of vastly uneven power, where one group can enforce its own interpretations of language onto the other. As Phil Bratta and Malea Powell have argued, cultural rhetorics is an emergent field that can take on such comparative analysis. This analysis "always requires an examination of issues of power, both those that arise within each cultural site of practice, and the power relations between the cultures involved in the comparative analysis" (Bratta and Powell 2016). The study of rhetoric as a Western phenomenon is not hospitable to sense making at the intersections of multiple identity categories and power dynamics. Yet these intersecting oppressions are crucial for understanding the inter-group relations from which rhetors make meaning in the off-reservation boarding school.

At Carlisle, PST accrued meaning during the assimilation period as settler society cast American Indians as culturally disabled in an attempt to justify a new wave of territorial expansion in the West. Indian educators enacted this colonial logic by creating a curriculum based on another group they viewed as communicatively disabled: the Deaf. The historical cultural rhetorics work I am doing here calls us to a constellated understanding of how different bodies and social identities are shaped and understood through language. Bridging so many categories of analysis—race, colonization, indigeneity, deafness, disability—is no easy task. But as scholars and teachers of writing, we do our work in an environment where theories of racial identity and disability influence literacy pedagogies. By engaging the history of English education as an assimilationist project, we can fight for a new paradigm that honors the culturally rich and expedient languages our students use to communicate as they enter unfamiliar rhetorical situations.

As deaf and Indigenous rhetors began to face assimilationist education, multilingual education thrived among other communities. Malathi Michelle Iyengar aargues that Western European immigrants were able to become citizens without surrendering their home languages because they fit the criteria of a "free white person" established in the 1790 Naturalization Act. In fact, bilingual public education for German students flourished from the 1830s through World War I (Iyengar 2014, 42). But for Richard Pratt, even European languages other than English presented a problem within the national boundaries of the United States. In his third annual report to the commissioner of Indian affairs in 1882, he wrote that "ignorance of our language is the greatest obstacle to the assimilation of the Indians with our population. It will be better for all when tribal names distinctions and languages are obliterated. The plan of exclusive schools for Germans was tried in the state of Pennsylvania and found to be foreign to the interest of the commonwealth in that it banded together a large mass of people to peculiar and special interest in each other rather than in the general welfare" (Report from Richard Henry Pratt 1882). Pratt articulates here a powerful organizing principle of the US nation-state—language is one of the only ways to bind together a group of people with disparate ethnic identities across an expansive geographic area. He considered federal laws that allowed immigrants to maintain their national tongues to be a failure of the government's responsibility. For Pratt, Native Americans in particular had to learn English because their languages threatened the racio-linguistic purity of the United States.

Post-bellum immigration laws demonstrate how the Deaf and Native Americans experienced similar challenges to their citizenship and full humanity because of their languages. Unlike other Western European immigrants, the Deaf were viewed as undesirable entrants to the United States. Douglas C. Baynton (2006, 383) writes that the Immigration Act of 1882 denied entry to any "lunatic, idiot, or person unable to take care of himself or herself without becoming a public charge." Deaf people were sent back to their countries of origin at US ports under the category of "person unable to take care of himself or herself." Baynton explains that Deaf people were "culturally defined as social dependents rather than social contributors," and eugenicists increasingly swayed policy with their view that the Deaf were "bearers of potentially defective heredity" (395). Like Native Americans, legally categorized as "domestic dependent nations" following the *Cherokee Nation v. Georgia* (1881) decision, Deaf people were considered insufficiently individualistic to enter the body of American citizenship. This notion of dependency characterized Native and Deaf cultures as childlike and created a paternalistic dynamic that the state exploited to institutionalize and educate these two groups.

While Pratt certainly believed in the linguistic purity of the nation, in other ways his racial views were out of step with the social evolutionism of his contemporaries. While social evolutionism takes a racialized—that is, fixed and biological—view of indigeneity, Pratt tended to embrace a much earlier notion of indigeneity as largely cultural—that is, mutable and subject to change through immersion in settler society.[2] Pratt's environmental views of indigeneity led him to dismiss the possibility of educating Native Americans with emancipated African Americans shortly after the Fort Marion prisoners arrived at Hampton. He quickly came to believe that Indians would benefit more from exposure to white families than from intermingling with African Americans. Pratt later summarized his views in his 1892 address "The Advantages of Mingling Indians with Whites." He said of enslaved Africans:

> They became English-speaking and civilized, because [they were] forced into association with English-speaking and civilized people; became healthy and multiplied, because they were property; and industrious,

because industry, which brings contentment and health, was a necessary quality to increase their value. Indians, on the other hand, remained savage, because [they were] forced back upon themselves and away from association with English-speaking and civilized people, and because of our savage example and treatment of them. (Pratt 1973, 263)

For Pratt, slavery benefited African Americans because it exposed them to English and habits of industry. The greater evil, he argued, was an Indian policy of removal, reservations, and war. We can see that Pratt's approach to Indian education emerged from his extreme views of environmental racial identity formation. For Pratt, Indians had to be exposed to settler culture. He viewed the off-reservation boarding school and slavery as parallel benevolent institutions because they had the potential to "civilize."

Pratt's inconsistent racial logics came into play in the early Carlisle curriculum. On the one hand, Pratt believed the students' very bodies were disabled by their language and culture—a social evolutionist view. On the other, Pratt (1973, 268) advanced his conviction that the Indian "is born a blank, like all the rest of us," characterizing students not through fixed, racial characteristics but through a mutable, cultural framework. If Indians were Lockean blank slates, then they could learn to be industrious Americans through education. This conviction shaped the school program in many ways. Students had to be taken away from their nations—as far away as possible—and they needed to spend time with white families on "outings," or long periods of farm labor away from school. Pratt's policies were shaped by the notion that "the way to break up the tribe was to break up the Indian family and to cultivate children's allegiance to the United States rather than to the tribe" (quoted in Piatote 2013, 5). By implementing a shared curriculum with schools for the Deaf, Pratt created the "blank slate" conditions that would allow his students to unlearn and relearn language, unlearn and relearn culture. If students could not speak but learned gestural language instead, they would be primed for full exposure to English without a trace of their previous linguistic knowledge. Any idiom or syntax from their native tongues would indicate that the students had not erased their cultural knowledge completely so they could start again as Euro-Americans. The project of destroying to replace would not be complete if students did not speak standard English.

There was a growing movement for standardization in the Deaf Education Movement as well. In the 1870s, deaf language and literacy education shifted from a bilingual/bicultural model known as manualism to an assimilationist model known as oralism. Like the Carlisle curriculum, oralism demanded embodied conformity to norms of an imagined standard English. Oralist schools would eliminate signing "by teaching only in speech, and by providing training in lip reading and articulation" (Edwards 2012, 184). Like Carlisle students, deaf students were forced to change their embodied language practices to fit within an imagined national ideal. In the manualist paradigm, deaf educators generally recognized signs as "the natural language of deaf people, both as the language that they most commonly used among themselves and as the language that originated from the deaf community itself" (Edwards 2012, 34). By coming together in large numbers for the first time in the missionary schools of the antebellum period, physically deaf people formed a Deaf community with its own language, culture, and values. These schools for the Deaf allowed students to develop their language without the attendant need for assimilation into standard spoken English.

By the 1870s, proponents of the oral method began to attack Deaf sign language. Prominent Deaf scholar and activist Paddy Ladd has referred to oralism as linguistic colonialism, a term that elegantly maps the parallels between Native and Deaf education in the Assimilation Era. Ten years before Pratt opened Carlisle, oralists were insisting that Deaf Americans pass as hearing. As Baynton (1996, 40) argues, "Sign language came to be seen as a language low in the scale of evolutionary progress, preceding in history even the most 'savage' of spoken languages and supposedly forming a link between the animal and the human." As early as 1844, Horace Mann and Samuel Gridley Howe pressed for the oral method. When Howe became chair of the Massachusetts Board of State Charities in 1863, he persuaded the state legislature to charter an oralist school. By 1880, a transatlantic congress of deaf educators (all hearing) committed itself to the Treaty of Milan, which stated that sign language restricted deaf children and should be replaced by oral training (Branson and Miller 2002, 43). Like Native students, the Deaf were forced to abandon their literacy practices to perform the dominant mode of language in America—standard English.

This overlapping history of post-bellum Indian and deaf education demonstrates how the concept of disability stripped Native Americans of their languages as the concept of the Indian savage was stripping Deaf Americans of their languages. The overlap between the understanding of Deaf and Native literacies shows how, as Jay Dolmage (2014) has argued, power circulates through communication.[3] The shifting curriculum at schools for the Deaf and Carlisle further demonstrates how cultural meanings of literacy can radically shape human beings' experiences and worldviews (Duffy 2007, 193–200). Indigenous and deaf sign languages threatened the racio-linguistic purity of the United States, and literacy education began to demand monolingual, spoken, and standardized English. The legacy of that standardization retains its power today. Despite language revitalization movements in both Native and Deaf communities, literacy education remains stubbornly reliant on a standard English paradigm in which difference is a problem to be solved rather than a basic characteristic of all communication to be embraced.

PLAINS SIGN TALK AS SURVIVANCE

To enact an English-only curriculum, the first off-reservation boarding school made an imagined hierarchy of literacy real. Reformers used social evolutionism to justify colonial desires for land and a monocultural society. These colonial impulses materialized in English classrooms where teachers were throwing sponges and teaching object lessons. Carlisle teachers produced linguistic disability in their students by stripping them of their rich communicative forms and then treating them as if they had used flawed communicative practices all along. To standardize has historically meant to diminish a student's available means of communication. Native students persistently refused to submit to the Carlisle curriculum that would diminish rather than enhance their ability to sustain good relations between their words and their nations. Gerald Vizenor's (1994) term *survivance* combines survival and resistance. It characterizes how Native American cultural identities persist in the face of colonial violence. At Carlisle, students used Plains Sign Talk to take advantage of their teachers' linguistic biases and push back against the curriculum that sought to strip them of their rhetorical power.

In spite of how hard Pratt and his teachers worked to block students from using their languages, students continued to communicate in their native tongues. Two years after teachers implemented their English-only curriculum, Stephen K. White Bear wrote about the persistent use of Siouxian languages in his composition "Speak Only English." The piece opens with White Bear explaining why he has been "talking Indian," so it is likely that he was assigned this essay as a punishment. He writes:

> I hear everybody talk Indian. So I suppose that is the reason I have been talking my own language but [a] great many of the boys say only the Sioux boys talk Indian continually but I don't believe them because I hear the other tribes talk Indian too but every boy and girl would like to know how to talk Sioux very much. They do not learn the English language they seem to want to know how to talk Sioux and I know some of them have been to school about eight years or six years but they do not learn so very

fast and they do not want to speak English they just want to know how to talk Sioux. (White Bear 1882, 4)

Because the majority of the first students came from the Rosebud and Pine Ridge agencies in South Dakota, Lakota would have been the most commonly spoken language between 1879 and 1883. It is clear that this has become a privileged language among the students at the school, with many wanting to learn Lakota more than English. This trend has come to the attention of the teachers, and they have assigned Stephen White Bear a composition as a punishment and to make him an example for the other students so they will stop "talking Indian" as well.

Later in the composition, White Bear (1882, 4) reveals that students have also continued to use Plains Sign Talk: "So many boys who are trying to speak only English they do not speak out in the English. They just use signs to each other they looks like a sick man they don't hold their heads up they hold their heads down continually." I read this moment as evidence that students are using PST covertly to talk to each other and block the teachers from understanding what they are saying. They can easily explain their use of signs, which have been previously endorsed by their teachers as preferable to their spoken languages. The teachers may view this gestural language as evidence of disability—"they looks like a sick man"—but signing has been an important part of Pratt's curriculum, and students have strategically continued to use Plains Sign Talk to communicate within the constraints of the total institution where they are detained.

Plains Sign Talk at Carlisle is a sophisticated rhetoric of relations. Students know that their teachers interpret PST as an unsophisticated series of gestures. They use this misinterpretation of an intertribal communication system to keep their rhetorical practices alive and to communicate in secret. The intertribal affordances of PST demonstrate how Pan-Indian relations emerge from a school that aims to stamp out such forms of political relationality. According to Kay Yandell (2012, 536), while PST "served to protect privacy between the two signers within earshot but out of sight of others, it also functioned to relay messages throughout or across a group." Plains Sign Talk allowed students to communicate privately with one another or share information quickly across the entire group without their teachers understanding what they were saying. It was also widely used by children as part of their everyday communication (535). Students from the Southern Plains have known and used this language for many years, so it is a commonality they share in addition to English, which might otherwise serve as their primary means of inter-group communication. Their teachers have unwittingly endorsed these covert communications in their English-only environment because they failed to understand PST as a communicative system with the same level of complexity as English. Carlisle students took advantage of their teachers' low cultural expectations of them to maintain and enhance their intertribal rhetorical relations. Because they would certainly have been punished for "speaking Sioux," sign talk was a powerful method of survivance for Carlisle's earliest students.

Another indication that students continued to covertly use their languages and subvert their education appears in Pratt's report at the end of the school's first three-year term. On September 30, 1882, he writes that "three years in school is not education and judgments based upon the success or failure of those who have made this mere beginning can only be imperfect" (Report from Richard Henry Pratt to Commissioner of Indian Affairs Hiram Price). As he attempts to manage the US Indian Bureau's expectations, we note a hesitancy in his usually bombastic prose. Pratt knows that many students are returning home without achieving the full measure of "civilization" he had hoped for. He also writes that the classroom motto has become "make haste slowly," another indication that the promise of the three-year language transformation has turned out to take longer than expected. Perhaps the delay is due to the students who continue to "speak Indian" or those who have decided to learn Lakota as well as English or those who use Plains Sign Talk to communicate privately with one another. It seems that most students are not speaking standardized English as they prepare to return home. In fact, many may be speaking new Indigenous languages as well.

Hazel W. Hertzberg (1971, 18) has argued that twentieth-century Pan-Indian movements emerged from off-reservation boarding schools. At Carlisle, Native students from dozens of tribes met one another and gained exposure to Lakota and Plains Sign Talk for the first time. These languages made new rhetorical relations possible as they became shared strategies for surviving the boarding school experience and resisting the English-only curriculum. Linguist William Leap (1993, 162, original emphasis) has written that Indian student varieties of English were "*codes under construction*, codes students were creating, as individuals and as a group, on the basis of the knowledge of language they had acquired in their home/tribal communities, were learning from their teachers, and were learning from each other." While teachers believed they were destroying Indigenous languages and replacing them with English, students were creating new rhetorical and linguistic relations for a new era of Indigenous survivance. When students used these languages strategically and at great risk of punishment, they sowed the seeds of Indigenous resistance for the twentieth century.

3

LAKOTA STUDENTS' EMBODIED
RHETORICS OF REFUSAL

This chapter examines the embodied rhetorics of a student named Ernest White Thunder within a larger context of Lakota rhetorics of refusal to allotment policies of the 1880s. Ernest was among the first group of students to come to Carlisle from the Sicangu Oyate, or Burnt Thigh, Nation at the Rosebud Agency in South Dakota. He entered school at age eighteen and went on a hunger strike to resist both the Carlisle curriculum and his captivity away from his homeland. When he tried and failed to run away, Ernest began to refuse everything: wearing his military uniform, writing, speaking in English, taking medicine, and, finally, eating. By framing the study of rhetoric as the art of persuasion, we tend to focus on a set of communicative strategies that most expediently bring about a desired result. But as Audra Simpson has argued, Indigenous refusal is not expedient—it is a set of tactics without a predefined set of goals or outcomes. For Indigenous nations, refusal is better understood as "the phenomenon of people thinking and acting as nationals in a scene of dispossession" (Simpson 2014, 33). Ernest White Thunder refused to abandon his national identity in the face of overwhelming colonial pressure. He used his body to communicate that refusal when all other forms of resistance failed. In so doing, Ernest modeled a rhetoric of refusal that would ignite further resistance by his nation as its people came to terms with the deaths of their children. This resistance would take many forms, including petitions, letters, and further embodied acts that came into relation with Ernest's hunger strike to open new possibilities for the Lakota to demand their sovereign rights to land and language.

Like many of Carlisle's first students, Ernest was the son of a leader who agreed to participate in Pratt's project so his children would learn English. Many believed that if their children learned English, they would return home and assist in ongoing negotiations with the US government over land rights. When Pratt traveled to the Dakotas in 1878, he did so in the context of massive loss of life and land for the Lakota people.

DOI: 10.7330/9781646420872.c003

The federal government annexed the sacred Black Hills following the Black Hills War of 1876 and continued to challenge the 1868 Fort Laramie Treaty that guaranteed Oceti Sakowin territory and hunting grounds, including the Great Sioux Reservation. As settlers continued to encroach on the boundaries of the reservation, violent conflict was ongoing. Although Pratt promised that Carlisle would provide the Lakota and the Dakota with the means to maintain their lands, the US Department of War had its own clearly stated motivations for bringing children east. Secretary of the Interior Carl Schurz viewed the children as "hostages for the good behavior of their people," replicating the strategy undertaken with the prisoners of war at Fort Marion a few years earlier (Pratt 1964, 220).

Ernest White Thunder's rhetoric of refusal accrues meaning within a continuum of refusals engaged by the Oceti Sakowin confederacy, and the Sicangu Oyate in particular, as they attempted to maintain their traditional lands and buffalo-hunting territories. Ernest's resistance reverberated as the US government pursued its effort to break up the 32-million-acre Great Sioux Reservation between the 1868 treaty and the signing of the 1889 Sioux Agreement. His hunger strike and suicide also connect him with a broader history of Indigenous embodied resistance as exemplified by the suicides of Cheyenne leaders Gray Beard and Lean Bear at Fort Marion. This chapter reads embodied rhetorical strategies in relation to Indigenous media and alphabetic texts to show how bodies are *written about* in the alphabetic archive but also how that archive alone cannot account for the tactics of Lakota nationals in what Simpson (2014) would call "a scene of dispossession." Ernest White Thunder's embodied rhetorics of refusal illuminate the problems with privileging alphabetic text. By reading Ernest's embodied refusals in the context of other tactics that take material form in x-marks, postscripts, collective authorship of petitions, trial transcripts, and literary essays, I argue for a capacious rhetoric of relations in which embodied, oral, and alphabetic communication materialize Lakota survivance in the face of colonial violence and coercion in the Assimilation Era.

The rhetoric of relations emerges here as an assemblage of tactics—embodied, textual, and material—the Oceti Sakowin used to delay or push back against the overwhelming force of a federal government set on breaking up their remaining reservation lands into privately owned allotments. These rhetorics also contribute to a growing body of scholarship that centers the body as an understudied site of rhetorical expression. Jay Dolmage (2009, 1) has argued that in rhetorical studies "we have accepted an historical narrative in which rhetoric . . .

denounces the body, overlooks its phenomenological and persuasive importance, and lifts discourse from its corporeal hinges." Certainly, an approach that denounces the body would fail to account for Ernest White Thunder's actions as rhetorical—that is, persuasive, influential, or world shaping. One result of such a limited frame has been a general lack of scholarly attention to the off-reservation boarding school period that is only now being corrected. Indeed, if we confine our analysis to Carlisle students' writing, rhetorics of survivance will not be immediately apparent due to the surveillance students faced and the ways Pratt used students as conduits for his own editorializing. Kathleen Washburn (2012, 381) has identified a similar issue in her study of the publications of the Society of American Indians, an archive that has been largely ignored "because of the group's association with the national project of assimilating Indigenous people to a rigid domestic order in the early twentieth century." The embodied rhetorics of Carlisle students correct the false narrative that Indians were complicit in their own erasure. These rhetorics demonstrate how Carlisle students understood themselves as representatives of their nations continuing the fight to maintain their sovereignty. Ernest's body speaks through his self-starvation while he lives. After his death, his body continues to represent an injustice the colonial government cannot erase.

Let me pause with a note on the language I use to describe Ernest and his nation. In Euro-American archival materials such as newspapers and letters, Ernest and the children who arrived with him at Carlisle are described as Sioux. When I use this term, it is to quote directly from or make reference to the worldview of Pratt, the US government, and late nineteenth-century settler society more generally. However, as Nick Estes (2019, 69) writes, "the Dakota, Nakota, and Lakota never called themselves 'Sioux'—that term derives from an abbreviation of 'Nadouessioux,' a French adoption of the Ojibwe word for 'little snakes' denoting the Ojibwe's enemies to its west. Instead, they simply called themselves the 'Oyate,' the 'Nation,' or the 'People', and sometimes the 'Oyate Luta' (the Red Nation); as a political confederacy, they called themselves the 'Oceti Sakowin Oyate' (The Nation of the Seven Council Fires)." As I explore how the Oceti Sakowin negotiated their territorial rights with the US government, I center the language of these nations whenever possible. As most of the rhetors in this chapter are members of the Sicangu Oyate, or Lakota-speaking Burnt Thigh Nation, this will be the most frequent identifier I use to situate Ernest, his father, and the other leaders and community members who engage with each other and the federal government in the fight for their children's return following Ernest's death.

Ernest White Thunder, or Wica-karpa (Knocked-It-Off),[1] was among the first eighty-two students to arrive at Carlisle. They disembarked from a train at midnight on October 5, 1879. Ernest's father, Chief White Thunder, was a leader at the Rosebud Agency in South Dakota. This reservation was the largest contributor of students in Carlisle's early years when Pratt depended on tribal leaders for recruits. In 1879, Pratt traveled to the Lakota Rosebud and Pine Ridge agencies to meet with Chiefs Spotted Tail (Sinte Gleska) and Red Cloud (Mahpiya Luta), respectively. These men were wary interlocutors. Spotted Tail was the uncle of Crazy Horse and witness to General William S. Harney's massacre of 86 Sicangus—half of them women and children—in 1855. The events of that day cemented his resolve for self-defense and survival, and he became known for taking the path of diplomacy throughout many conflicts with US forces (Estes 2019, 99). Red Cloud, too, emerged as a leader following cruelty and violence waged by US soldiers. After Colonel John M. Chivington and his soldiers massacred 200 peaceful Cheyennes at Sand Creek in Colorado in 1863, Red Cloud led an alliance of Cheyennes, Lakotas, Arapahos, and Dakotas on campaigns to take back their buffalo-hunting grounds (Estes 2019, 105). Pratt did not want to meet with the Lakota either. He hoped to recruit students from the Cheyenne, Arapaho, Kiowa, and Comanche agencies because he had connections with these groups from his previous assignments, Fort Marion in particular. But Indian commissioner Hyde insisted that Pratt begin his recruitment with the Lakota to subdue resistance to their confinement in ever-shrinking reservations (Pratt 1964, 220).

According to Pratt's (1964, 222) account, Spotted Tail conferred with the other chiefs at Rosebud and said "the white people are all thieves and liars . . . we are not going to give any children to learn such ways." He referenced the 1868 Fort Laramie Treaty, which the United States systematically violated, eventually confiscating 7.7 million acres of the Lakota's sacred Black Hills and creating several small reservations, including Rosebud, by 1877. The treaty stipulated a permanent reservation of 32 million acres with a vast expanse of hunting grounds that extended Oceti Sakowin territory to 70 million acres total (Estes 2019, 108). In initial treaty negotiations, Red Cloud insisted that the treaty was "not just an agreement between two human nations, but also an agreement among the nonhuman ones as well—including the buffalo nations" (quoted in Estes 2019, 109). Relations between the Lakota and the Buffalo nations were foundational to Red Cloud's negotiations with the federal government. By the time Pratt came to confer with Red Cloud in 1879, the United States had waged genocidal war on those

Buffalo nations, and the strategic path forward for the Lakota people was very much in question. A strong desire to restore good relations on their homeland helps explain why Lakota parents sent their children many miles to the east to learn English.

Understanding on some level the extreme changes the Lakota were experiencing, Pratt told Spotted Tail that they needed to educate their children to avoid being further misled by whites. He recalls asking, "Cannot you see, Spotted Tail, what a disadvantage you and your people are under" (Pratt 1964, 224). Spotted Tail agreed to send five of his sons, and other chiefs including Ernest's father sent their children as well. Ernest White Thunder thus became many things—a hostage of the US government, a leader's child who needed to set an example, the stake on whom White Thunder would continue to claim authority among his people, and the hope for a new generation that could convince the US government to honor their treaty agreements. White Thunder hoped his son would learn the language of Euro-Americans to help his nation survive.

We know nothing about Ernest White Thunder from his own writing because his writing does not appear in the archival record; his refusal to write does. Ernest arrived in Carlisle in October 1879. By February 1880, it was clear that he would not be the exemplary student his father had hoped for. Pratt wrote to the chief about Ernest's bad behavior, and White Thunder wrote back: "My son: I want to tell you one thing. You did not listen to the school teacher, and for that reason you were scolded . . . At this agency there are over 7000 people and there are four chiefs. These chiefs sent their children to school and others followed their lead" (Letter from Chief White Thunder to Ernest White Thunder, April 1880). White Thunder asked his son to write home a letter in English and reminded him: "I said if it takes five or ten years, if you did not learn anything you should not come back here." He closed with another encouragement for Ernest to write: "Your grandfather and mother would be glad to hear from you if you can write a word in English." Pratt reprinted this letter in the school's publicity newspaper, the *Eadle Keatah Toh*, as it was his common practice to publicly scold students for bad behavior. Pratt added his commentary to the letter, writing that Ernest "has been exceptionally idle, and sometimes disobedient." He continued: "When asked by his teacher to whom he would write the letter which each student is required to send home at the close of the month, he replied with the utmost nonchalance, 'I have no friends to write to; I had an aunt once, but the bears eat her up.'" These are the only words attributed to Ernest White Thunder that remain in the alphabetic archive.

Figure 3.1. Portrait of Ernest White Thunder (Knocks Off) and his aunt Agnes (White Cow) posed on the steps of the bandstand on the Carlisle school grounds. Photo by John N. Choate, ca. 1879, shortly after Ernest arrived at the school. To avoid writing letters home in English, Ernest later claimed he had no family and that his aunt had been eaten by a bear. Courtesy, Cumberland County Historical Society, Carlisle, PA.

Ernest reveals himself to be what Gerald Vizenor calls a postindian warrior. He "ousts the inventions [of the Indian] with humor, new stories, and the simulations of survivance" (Vizenor 1994, 5). "I have no friends to write to; I had an aunt once, but the bears eat her up." With this retort, Ernest White Thunder performs a kind of primitive Indian identity within the fantasy world of his white audience—he frames his childhood as wild and dangerous, in which bears are eating his relatives. And yet it is impossible to take him seriously; he is turning the idea of an Indian childhood on its head, mocking the beliefs of his teachers and showing them for what they are—thinly veiled fairy tales to justify colonial violence. Indeed, as Malea Powell (2002, 405) has argued, rhetorics of survivance emerge when Indigenous rhetors consume and reproduce nineteenth-century beliefs about Indians to produce something else—a new means of performing Indianness to survive changing conditions of colonial dominance. As figure 3.1 demonstrates, Ernest White Thunder's aunt was a student at Carlisle, so his comment is even more ridiculous.[2] Ernest's rhetoric of survivance involves verbally mocking his teachers' beliefs about Indians even as he actively refuses to take on the trappings of settler society—alphabetic English literacy in particular.

Ernest felt pressure from all sides to learn to write English and perform other behaviors such as speaking English only, wearing a uniform, performing work industriously, and running military drills with the other boys. He wanted to go home and wrote telling his family so but discovered that he could not return unless he succumbed to Pratt's demands. It must have been a harsh blow to hear from his father that five to ten years might pass and, even worse, to know that his father's leadership position overshadowed his son's pleas. Further, Ernest was experiencing a break with his homeland. As Jacqueline Fear-Segal and Susan D. Rose (2016, 2) have argued, boarding schools traumatized Native students because their "physical and spiritual wellbeing was anchored not just within their communities, but also within the environment and land that surrounded them." Despite the benevolent explanations Pratt gave Spotted Tail and White Thunder for the boarding school location, he knew exactly how damaging it would be for Lakota children to be displaced. The 1,500 miles between South Dakota and Pennsylvania were intended to facilitate the total loss of tribal language and culture. Ernest experienced this violent separation, and he refused to accept it as the means to a greater end.

Following the public shame of seeing his father's rebuke in print, Ernest amplified his refusals. When his letter failed to generate the desired result, Ernest refused to write home at all. He claimed to have no friends or family, a reaction no doubt to a perceived betrayal by his father. Pratt minimized Ernest's acts of resistance, seeing only a non-compliant student fabricating a story about an aunt eaten by a bear. In fact, Ernest had engaged with writing at Carlisle within a relational framework—as a way to communicate with his family and bring about his return home. His father's answer certainly violated Ernest's sense of being a good relative—or adhering to the Lakota philosophy of Mitákuye Oyás'iŋ, meaning "all my relations" or "we are all related" (Estes 2019, 15). When Ernest says he "has no friends to write to," he may well be communicating the dissolution of his sense of right relations with his family and his nation.

Ernest fought the English-only curriculum as best he could. He refused to engage when that curriculum demanded his bodily, mental, and affective obedience to norms of Euro-American culture. To maintain kinship ties, students had to write in English. But doing so put strains on families already separated by a great distance. The letters home required Indian agents to translate the words of students to parents and then parents' words back to English for students. Letters were then read and screened by Pratt and Carlisle teachers before getting back to students. All of this mediation ultimately allowed Pratt to oversee and respond to what students and parents wrote to each other. It further placed Native parents at the margins of communication with their children, breaking an affective and pedagogical bond that reproduced culture, language, and kinship relations. When Ernest claimed he had no family, he blocked Pratt's ability to control him through manipulation of communication. He took his words out of the circuit of Pratt's curriculum, government agents, and his parents' words in translation.

Mark Rifkin has shown that Pratt manipulated kinship ties to bring about the larger government policy of allotment, which sought to break down Native communal formations of land ownership. He explains, "Land tenure, subsistence, and residency [were] reorganized in ways that [broke] down extended social networks and [broke] up shared territories and in which affective ties [were] rerouted from larger communal formation to the nuclear family" (Rifkin 2006, 32). Through his pedagogy of letter writing and later outing his students to Pennsylvania farms to observe and serve white families, Pratt hoped tribal ties would be replaced by the individualized single-family model. While Ernest did not live long enough to experience the outing program, he did witness Pratt's early attempts to dissolve tribal bonds and force his students into new affective relations modeled in Euro-American individualism.

Ernest's refusal to write progressed to other bodily expressions of refusal that would eventually end his life. Chief White Thunder visited with a delegation from Rosebud in the spring of 1880. The visit prompted Spotted Tail to withdraw his children from the school when he was horrified to see them performing military drills like white soldiers and found that his son had been punished by being locked in the guard house for days. But Chief White Thunder was unbending. He would not take his son home.

As a hostage of the US government, Ernest had very few options, which became clear to him when his attempts to control his fate failed.

As the Lakota delegation boarded a train to head west, Ernest hid onboard but was discovered in Harrisburg and sent back to Carlisle (Adams 1995, 126). He refused to stay at school but was powerless to leave. Running away was a tactic used by many boarding school students after Ernest, although he may have been the first to attempt it. In their survey of American Indian boarding school experiences, Margaret Archuleta, Brenda J. Child, and K. Tsianina Lomawaima (2000, 47) write that "when friction or homesickness became unbearable, students in every boarding school across Canada and the United States reached the same resolution and ran away." Indeed, Ernest's act of resistance reaches both forward and backward in time when placed within a continuum of Indigenous resistance to captivity. The Kiowa escape plot I explore in chapter 1 is one example. The resonance of this shared act of running away is so powerful that contemporary Native American writers often feature running away from boarding school in their works. A very few examples include Louise Erdrich in her poem "Indian Boarding School: The Runaways" and her novel *LaRose*, where the main character, Landreaux Iron, and his friend Romeo run away from their boarding school at Fort Totten in North Dakota. Leslie Marmon Silko's novel *Gardens in the Dunes* tells the story of a runaway—Indigo of the fictional Sand Lizard people—from the Sherman Institute in Riverside, California. Running away is a shared rhetorical strategy students used to refuse to engage in assimilationist education and its attendant spatial dislocation from their homelands and communities. Running away registers resistance and, even when unsuccessful, lends a sense of hope and possibility to those who plan to run away and those who witness their peers running away. When Ernest ran away, he communicated that he was not powerless to act.

Ernest's final refusals resulted in his death. In mid-December 1880, Pratt reported to Washington that Ernest was very sick because he refused to eat. Pratt wrote on December 6: "He is still very obstinate [and] seems to rather want to die" (quoted in Adams 1995, 128). A few days later, Pratt wrote to Chief White Thunder informing him that his son was dead. His letter explained, "I had to make him go to the hospital and had to take his clothes away from him to keep him in bed. He would not eat and he would not take medicine unless I made him and then he would spit it out" (128). Ernest's self-starvation had lasted around two months (Fear-Segal and Rose 2016, 188). This student turned to the semiotics of desperation we recognize today as hunger striking. As Maud Ellman (1993, 17) has argued, "Self-starvation is all about performance." It is a spectacle that shames the oppressor and creates sympathy and solidarity with an outraged audience, in this case the fellow students and later the members of their nation when they learn of Ernest's death (17). Just as Lean Bear refused to eat at Fort Marion to maintain his warrior identity and inspire the continued resistance of the other prisoners, Ernest used his body to resist the captivity forced upon him by the US government.

An 1878 action by incarcerated Russian dissidents is generally considered the first hunger strike in the contemporary sense of the term, where a single activist or group of activists starve themselves to bring attention to their cause (Lurie 2019). Lean Bear's death in 1875 and Ernest White Thunder's death in 1880 do not fully conform to the contemporary understanding of a hunger strike—for example, they could not make a public declaration of their decision to stop eating—but their self-starvation adds a necessary corrective to our understanding of hunger striking as political and resistant rhetoric. Indeed, many scholarly accounts of hunger striking fail to acknowledge self-starvation and suicide as Indigenous tactics of resistance to colonial domination. In the case of Lean Bear, his primary audience was the other prisoners whom he inspired to continue resisting despite their captivity and in ways that would disrupt the notion that their captors held complete power over their bodies. For Ernest, self-starvation was a way to refute the Carlisle narrative of benevolence and make clear that the school was not educating students to support their nations against colonial incursion but rather working in concert with the federal government to destroy the future of their nations. In 2012, Chief Theresa Spence of the Attawapiskat First Nation went on a hunger strike to force a dialogue about treaty implementation between Algonquians and the Canadian government in Ottawa. Her six-week hunger strike forced a meeting of First Nations leaders, the prime minister, and the governor general while galvanizing the Idle No More movement in the ongoing fight for Indigenous sovereignty in Ottawa (Tomiak 2016, 15–16). Ernest White Thunder's rhetoric of refusal places him within the broader context of Indigenous embodied resistance. When he ran away from school and refused to eat, he participated in a tactic to uphold treaty relations and national sovereignty within a new context of colonial dispossession.

An important similarity between Ernest's hunger strike and that of twentieth- and twenty-first-century hunger strikers is how they all use starvation to make explicit the immorality of their captors or opponents. British and American suffragists engaged in hunger striking while incarcerated, as did Bobby Sands for Irish independence, Mahatma Gandhi for Indian independence, César Chávez for farm workers' rights, Nelson

Mandela to protest apartheid, and prisoners at Guantanamo Bay to protest their indefinite captivity without trial. While Ernest White Thunder did not hunger strike in the formalized or public way we currently recognize, his resistance brought forward political and moral claims in ways that resonate with these later examples. As Stephen J. Scanlan, Laurie Cooper Stoll, and Kimberly Lumm (2015, 277) have argued, the hunger strike is "a nonviolent tactic of last resort indicating the intensity of the injustice being protested, and in many cases the lack of other available tactics." Ernest exhausted all of his other means to leave Carlisle before turning to hunger—a last resort indeed. The detainees at Guantanamo Bay share many material conditions with the Fort Marion prisoners and Carlisle students, as their detention is part of a military strategy that is expedient for the US government and justified to the American public as an issue of national well-being. Marouf Hasian Jr. (2014, 345) argues that the Guantanamo detainees craft "subaltern rhetorics" that interrogate the military ideologies of dehumanization and human rights violations at Guantanamo Bay. So, too, does Ernest White Thunder interrogate the US government's fantasy of benevolence when he shows Carlisle for what it is—a site of colonial violence organized around settler greed for territory. Leah Montange's study of a hunger strike by immigrants in a detention center in Tacoma, Washington, in 2014 provides another uncomfortable contemporary resonance with the Carlisle and Fort Marion sites. She illuminates how a hunger strike can foster "relationships of solidarity between inside and outside the detention . . . political relationships among detainees as well as among supporters" (Montange 2017, 511). When Ernest engaged in a hunger strike to death, an extreme version of self-starvation also deployed by Sands and Gandhi, his death became politically significant to his peers and his nation. His death would resonate for decades as the Lakota formulated resistance to attempts by the United States to erase their nation, language, and land claims.

On the way to Fort Marion, Gray Beard and Lean Bear made their deaths a spectacle to lend courage to the other prisoners. Ernest's peers were also witness to his suffering and grief-stricken by his death. Luther Standing Bear wrote that as he and the other Lakota boys first traveled to Carlisle, they thought they were on their way to die at the hands of white people. He recalls that the older boys "sang brave songs so that we would all meet death according to the Lakota code—fearlessly" (Standing Bear 2016a, 217). Ernest's decision to stop eating and ultimately to die resonates with these boys' hopes. Ernest communicated his willingness to die bravely to circulate a greater message for his peers at school and his relatives at home. His hunger strike, when viewed as an embodied rhetoric of relations, shows how Ernest re-inscribed the value of his life as part of the national collective that would survive beyond his death and beyond the immediacy of conditions at Carlisle.

Ernest refused to write, refused to stay at Carlisle, refused to be a student, refused to stay in bed, and, finally, refused to eat. These refusals speak volumes as we try to understand what it meant to learn to write in English at the Carlisle Indian Industrial School. Ernest shows that writing itself became an assault on his identity and his relations to home and nation. As his actions appeared in letters between his father and Pratt and then in the school periodical for all to see, Ernest recognized how the US government used alphabetic literacy as a colonial technology. When he refused to engage with alphabetic literacy, Ernest practiced a strategy of resistance that would carry through into other modes. He used his body to signify the impossibility of his rhetorical situation—he could not be a Sicangu boy and survive at the off-reservation school. In Ernest's case, the written archive is woefully insufficient. To make sense of his resistant rhetoric, a method that accounts for the written record in relation to embodied and extra-textual rhetorical tactics is needed. Ernest's story shows how embodied acts are a powerful communicative tool for students resisting the cultural expectations imposed on them by the powerful.

BODIES, TREATIES, X-MARKS

Ernest White Thunder died on December 13, 1880. That same day, another child from the Rosebud Agency named Maude Little Girl died from pneumonia (Landis 2016, 188). They were not the first children to die at Carlisle—a Dakota boy, Amos LaFramboise, and a Cheyenne boy, Abe Lincoln, had died shortly after arriving at the school. But the deaths of two Rosebud children on the same day led to heightened outrage, especially because Ernest's death could not be easily explained by Pratt. To make matters worse, another child from Rosebud died a mere month later. On January 19, 1881, Dennis Strikes First, son of Sicangu headman Blue Tomahawk, succumbed to typhoid pneumonia. These deaths would reverberate for many years as their parents and relatives grieved, demanded their children's remains, and transformed their grief into petitions for the return of all the children they had sent to Carlisle.

The deaths transformed the lives of Carlisle students as well. Pratt wrote to Maude's father, Swift Bear, that "the teachers and the scholars all loved Maud [*sic*] and their hearts are full of grief because she is dead.

The Sioux girls cried all night" (quoted in Adams 1995, 130). Writing about Ernest's death, Luther Standing Bear (2006b, 159) recalled, "that was one of the hard things about our education—we had to get used to so many things we had never known before that it worked on our nerves to such an extent that it told on our bodies." Standing Bear's recollection of his embodied reaction to Ernest's death stands in contrast to the writing he did at Carlisle, which gives the impression that he embraced the school's mission. One such example is a letter to his father in 1882 in which he reacts to the death of another Sioux boy named Alvan. In the letter, he explains that Alvan is in heaven now "because he was a good boy everywhere" and asks his father to "give up [the] Indian way" and "believe God, obey him and pray to Him" (quoted in Emery 2017, 45). Standing Bear's school writings stand in stark contrast to his embodied experience as reported in later reflections, speaking to how students could and did express in their bodies what they could not express in spoken or written language at the school.

To understand the experiences of the first students to attend Carlisle, it is crucial to remember that these children watched their friends and relatives die slowly from institutional diseases like tuberculosis and pneumonia. Ernest's slow death must have been horrible to witness as well, and Luther Standing Bear describes that experience by suggesting that his own body, indeed, the bodies of all the students, were affected by Ernest's death. The rhetorical power of a hunger strike as well as its effect on the audience becomes clear in Standing Bear's memory of how Ernest's death "told on our bodies." Ernest White Thunder's embodied rhetoric of refusal circulated through the memory of his nation for years, ultimately shaping the future of Lakota-US relations and providing a catalyst for further resistance.

In this section, I discuss the ways the Lakota transformed their grief into petitionary rhetoric that mirrored Ernest's rhetoric of refusal. Almost a decade later, in 1888, Richard Pratt came to the Dakotas to secure signatures for the Dawes Bill, which would break up the Great Sioux Reservation into smaller reservations and individual allotments, opening millions of acres to white settlement. While unified resistance did not outlast the coercive tactics of General George Crook the next year, it was clear that the deaths of Ernest White Thunder and other children impacted resistance against Pratt. Ernest's rhetoric of refusal ignited a collective response to the ways Carlisle tried to educate Lakota children out of their language and their claims to land. When Ernest went on a hunger strike and died, he envisioned a collective survivance beyond the limits of his own life. Ernest's body and the bodies of other children who died at Carlisle would continue to circulate and make meaning as a primary source of conflict that hindered ongoing attempts by the United States to shift territorial boundaries.

Following the deaths of Maude, Ernest, and Dennis, a series of letters and petitions circulated among Pratt, Commissioners of Indian Affairs Rowland Trowbridge and Hiram Price,[3] and the relatives of the children from the Rosebud Agency. These letters demonstrate the competing cultural logics and rhetorical tactics Pratt and the Sicangu leadership deployed to achieve their desired ends. By reading these letters through the frame I developed above as Ernest White Thunder's rhetoric of refusal, a pattern emerges in which Sicangu rhetors repeatedly refuse the conditions imposed on them by the Carlisle school through both textual and extra-textual means. While Ernest's resistance registers in the archival record only through textual reporting of his embodied acts, the letters between the Sicangu Oyate and the US government demonstrate how Indigenous rhetorics of refusal took material form in letters, x-marks, postscripts, and collective petitionary writing.

Immediately following Ernest's and Maude's deaths, Pratt wrote three letters to their parents and one letter to the commissioner of Indian affairs. His tried to explain the deaths and absolve himself of blame. He wrote first to White Thunder that his son had refused to eat or take medicine, and he wrote to Swift Bear that Maude had come to Carlisle with diseased lungs and died when the tuberculosis turned to pneumonia (Adams 1995, 129). Perhaps feeling that his initial letter to White Thunder was not sufficient, Pratt's writing grew more fraught—he wrote the first letter on December 14, the day after Ernest's death, and then another, longer letter on December 15 (Adams 1995, 128–129). In the second letter, Pratt attempts to explain Ernest's death as a good death in the context of Lakota beliefs:

> I look upon this detachment of children away from your people somewhat as you would upon a party sent out to gather a quantity of buffalo meat or even sent out to make war upon some other people or to capture horses from some other people. You know how that is my friend, how that very often there are some who never come back and such is the course of things in this life . . . Never in all the history of your tribe have you sent parties away from it on a better mission than this one. (quoted in Adams 1995, 129)

Comparing Ernest's death to a tragedy that occurs on a hunting or war party, Pratt suggests that the boy died for a cause larger than himself, a claim that resonates with Ernest's own ethos in his hunger strike. However, Pratt wants to shift the meaning of Ernest's death to shore up the morality of his educational project, a project Ernest explicitly rejected.

Because Ernest chose to die rather than succumb to assimilationist education, he undermines Pratt's narrative of innocence. Ernest brings Carlisle's colonial violence into view. Now Pratt must reach for increasingly frantic rhetorical means to re-inscribe his sense of moral purposes for bringing Indian children to Carlisle and keeping them there despite their worsening health.

It took a few days for these letters to reach Rosebud and another week for the parents' response to arrive in Washington. The next letter in the correspondence is dated December 27, 1880, and is transcribed by Agent Cook, the Indian agent at Rosebud (Letter from White Thunder and Swift Bear to Agent Cook). This letter is not addressed to Pratt but to the commissioner of Indian affairs, suggesting that the Sicangu leadership went above Pratt's head to seek redress for the deaths of their children. The letter asks that the children's remains be sent home to be buried in their ancestral lands. The letter is signed "White Thunder + Swift Bear for us—" and has a postscript signed by Spotted Tail. "For us" marks the collective voice of the letter. It is not only the fathers of the dead children who are responding but the entire community. Spotted Tail's additional signature is also significant. In this and other correspondence, he affixes his name to the collective signatories as an important leader whose voice carries extra weight in diplomatic negotiations.

This letter attempts to communicate the extraordinary grief the community is experiencing over the deaths of their children. The Sicangu at Rosebud write:

> They are gone from earth forever gone to join the others of our children in the land of the Great Spirit. The jewels are gone the caskets are only left and they are far very far away from us. We cannot bear to have them sleep so far away from their earthly home our hearts will grieve too long if we do not have what is left of them back to our homes. We want to dig their graves with our own hands. we want when the birds begin to sing + the flowers begin to bloom to have them where we can strew their graves with flowers and have them hear (in their spirits) the sweet songs of the "angel birds" that bathe around and about their quiet resting places. (Letter from White Thunder and Swift Bear to Agent Cook, December 27, 1880)

The writers engage the language of sentiment from the Euro-American tradition to appeal to the Indian commissioner while simultaneously emphasizing their connection to their homeland. Jewels, flowers, birds, and angels are all tropes from the nineteenth-century Euro-American cult of mourning, intended to petition the United States in its own language of national morality—an especially powerful rhetorical tactic, as sentimental literature glorifies the grave as a site of moral pedagogy for the

American nation (Klotz 2014, 337–338). The letter also reinforces the connection between the Sicangu children's national identity and their land base by repeating "land," "home," "earthly home," and how "far away" the children's bodies are from where they belong. By overlaying claims to their children's bodies with the language of sentiment, the Sicangu rhetors craft a diplomatic appeal to the federal government that claims to have benevolent intentions for their children's education and is further bound to educate the children by the terms of the 1868 treaty. White Thunder, Swift Bear, and their nation demand the return of their children while also shoring up their collective identity through group authorship and the language of homeland. This letter aims to restore right relations among nations, land, and kinship that have been thrown out of balance by Carlisle.

Spotted Tail dictates a separate postscript, which the agent transcribes up the side of the letter. This part of the letter is signed with only Spotted Tail's name. This section stands apart both materially, in that it is written sideways, and through the single signature. It reads, "Spotted Tail is present and desires to say to you that, he thinks when 'our children' get sick + the Dr. cannot help them they ought to be sent home—for if they are to die we want them to die at home. Spotted Tail" (Letter from White Thunder and Swift Bear to Agent Cook, December 27, 1880). The leader, famed for his diplomacy, takes a different space on the page for his own petitionary claims. He adds separate demands and lends authority to the collective communication. Spotted Tail, too, emphasizes the notion of home. The term appears twice in his short passage. Either Spotted Tail or the agent places "our children" in quotation marks, again emphasizing how the Sicangu children at Carlisle are part of a larger collective that takes responsibility for them. It is also worth noting that Spotted Tail's name appears twice, indicating that he asked the agent to highlight his speech as a leader and spokesperson for the larger community. Spotted Tail's postscript has the desired effect. After the deaths of Maude and Ernest, Pratt regularly sends sick children home to avoid having their deaths occur under his supervision.

While Pratt recognized the seriousness of the children's deaths and continued to make changes to his policies as a result, he did not send their remains home as the Sicangu demanded. Instead, he determined that the Rosebud Agency would benefit from material goods produced at Carlisle, such as wagons and tin ware. He thought sending these goods to the Rosebud Agency would remind the parents of why they had sent their children east. On January 26, 1881 (about a month after the letter from White Thunder and Swift Bear was written), Pratt wrote to the commissioner of Indian affairs. He suggested that sending goods would exert "a counter influence against the death[s] of White Thunder and Blue Tomahawk's sons and Swift Bear's daughter though I think these losses are philosophically accepted by them" (Letter from Richard Henry Pratt to the Commissioner of Indian Affairs). Pratt viewed the ongoing political crisis brought on by the children's deaths as a problem with a capitalist solution. He would send goods to make up for the losses of the children. Pratt's callous response would have decades of repercussions in ongoing negotiations between the United States and the Lakota. Luther Standing Bear recalls in his 1928 autobiography *My People the Sioux* (2006b, 159) that "White Thunder said he wanted the body of his son sent home, but if the school authorities would not do that, they might at least place a headstone over his grave. Neither request was ever granted." While the Sicangu engaged in intercultural negotiation for the return of their children in the sentimental language of their white audience, Pratt remained committed to his plan to turn Indians into Americans who valued property and industry above all else. His benevolent impulse shows itself as a fiction through his treatment of Ernest both before and after his death. Pratt would not be able to regain the trust of the Rosebud Lakota with wagons.

By the spring of 1881, the Sicangu refused to wait any longer for Pratt to honor their demands. They held a general council in early May to discuss the deaths of children at Carlisle. The council determined to demand that all of their children be sent home and that a school be built at the Rosebud Agency for their further education. On May 23, the council dictated a letter to Agent Cook and sent copies to the commissioner of Indian affairs, the secretary of the interior, Richard Pratt, and the president of the United States (Letter from Spotted Tail, Two Strike, White Thunder, and Swift Bear to Agent Cook). Much like the December letter, this document is signed collectively with the added formality of x-marks inscribed by Spotted Tail, Two Strike, White Thunder, and Swift Bear. Following the four x-marks, the letter is signed "and the council generally."

The letter communicates a power symmetry between the Sicangu and the United States, a rhetorical relation that attempts to bring about a political relation of equality between two nations bound by treaty agreements. The letter has four recipients and four x-mark signatories. As Scott Richard Lyons (2010, 3) has argued, the x-mark is "a contaminated and coerced sign of consent made under conditions that are not of one's making. It signifies power, agency, and a lack of agency. It is a decision one makes when something has already been decided for you, but it is still a decision . . . there is always the prospect of slippage, indeterminacy, unforeseen consequences, or unintended results; it is always possible, that is, that an x-mark could result in something good." Following Lyons, Amanda J. Zink (2015, 42) has characterized Native students' boarding school writings as x-marks, confined by the discursive context of the boarding school. The x-mark, then, is a rhetorical move that demonstrates how strategies overlap between students at school and their parents at home as they all continue to negotiate despite the power imbalance with the United States. In the case of this petition for the children's return, the council knows that a just outcome is unlikely. And yet the x-marks and every rhetorical move in the letter push toward indeterminacy—the possibility of something good. The x-mark on this petition calls on conventions of the x-mark on a treaty agreement; because this letter communicates the decision of a council held by the entire nation, we have further evidence that it is intended to recall the 1868 treaty agreement and remind the US government interlocutors that they are dealing with a sovereign nation.

The letter communicates the demands of one nation's leaders to another's as it addresses President Garfield and his cabinet. To draw further equivalence, the council writes: "We love our children just as dearly as the whites do theirs, it grieves our hearts when we hear they are sick and we mourn hard and long when they die and are taken away from us" (Letter from Spotted Tail, Two Strike, White Thunder, and Swift Bear to Agent Cook, May 23, 1881). The language, structure, and appeals in this letter formalize a relation of equivalence between the Sicangu and the United States. The letter concludes, "We ask you as you love and sympathize with us to send our children back to us and with them a school and teachers to educate them" (Letter from Spotted Tail, Two Strike, White Thunder, and Swift Bear to Agent Cook, May 23, 1881). A final claim to a shared affective bond between the nations serves as the closing equivalence claim. The Sicangu communicate in the strongest diplomatic terms, demanding their sovereign rights as equal to the United States with the additional language of sentiment around their pain and grief at the moral wrong Carlisle has done to them through the deaths of their children.

As in the earlier letter, Spotted Tail asks for a postscript, this time lending his name and authority while asking Agent Cook to write on the nation's behalf. The postscript reads:

> Spotted Tail has asked me to add a postscript to this letter and I do so very cheerfully. I have endeavored in every way to induce these Indians to keep their children where they are. The constant sickness and deaths at the

school of our children renders it extremely difficult to keep these Indians in good heart, and I do think as we sooner or later will have a school of our own it would be for the best interest of the agency and the Indians to comply with the request they have made. The mourning of those whose children have died is simply frightful. (Letter from Spotted Tail, Two Strike, White Thunder, and Swift Bear to Agent Cook, May 23, 1881)

Spotted Tail dictates the letter such that both his x-mark and his name appear in prominent places—the signature line as in a treaty document and the postscript as he presents himself as a leader with special authority to induce the agent to advocate for the nation. In the postscript, Agent Cook agrees that the children should be sent home and educated at an agency school. He also speaks to the mourning of the children's relatives, which he characterizes as "simply frightful." This appeal demonstrates that consensus has been built around the issue of the children's education—an essential aspect of Lakota decision making. The Sicangu leaders have demonstrated even the agent's agreement with the collective decision to demand the return of their children. The letter captures how a moment of crisis led the Sicangu Oyate to draw on their rhetorical and diplomatic repository to materialize their ongoing survival.

What happened next is not entirely clear because the correspondence in the extant archive between the Sicangu and the government ends after this letter, all four copies of which remain in the National Archives in Washington, DC. It is clear that Pratt did not give much weight to the Sicangu demands that their children be returned. In fact, he remembers the negotiation over Ernest's body very differently from either Luther Standing Bear's account or the distraught tone of the Rosebud petition. When a Zuni child, Frank Cushing, died in September 1881, his parents also demanded that his remains be sent home.[4] Pratt wrote to the Zuni Pueblo agent and the Indian commissioner that "it certainly would not be practicable to remove the body of this boy at present. It might be done after a while. White Thunder whose only son died at the school was very anxious to have his son's remains sent back to his home in Dakota. When he saw that we had him buried as our own dead are buried and the place marked, he said he was satisfied to have him stay here and he thought it was better" (Letter from Richard Henry Pratt to the Commissioner of Indian Affairs and B. M Thomas, September 30, 1881). Clearly, Pratt was manipulating the narrative of Ernest's death and the subsequent outrage at Rosebud to serve his own purposes—maintaining the status quo of procedures at Carlisle as well as his own authority to determine what would happen to the children both in life and after death.

Another reason the petition may ultimately have been ignored is that Spotted Tail died on August 5, 1881, shortly after the general council. Although the details of his death are contested, we know he was shot by Crow Dog, another Lakota leader. Spotted Tail's death likely contributed to the breakdown of communication between the Rosebud Agency and the government. Ultimately, the petition was not successful, and the Rosebud children stayed at Carlisle until their appointed three-year term ended in June of the next year (1882).

The breakdown of Sicangu resistance after Spotted Tail's death is best demonstrated by the return of his own children to Carlisle despite his clear and repeated objections to the school. Pratt used Spotted Tail's death to strengthen his own position. He wrote a letter to the Indian commissioner one week after Spotted Tail died, claiming he "was told by Secretary [Carl] Schurz that [Spotted Tail] had asked to return his children to the school and the Secretary said he had informed him that he might do so provided that he returned them at his own expense" (Letter from Richard Henry Pratt to the Commissioner of Indian Affairs, August 11, 1881). I am suspicious of this claim for a number of reasons. For one thing, Pratt is reporting third-hand information from Schurz that is at least a year old—he writes that this request occurred "last year at this time." In addition, Spotted Tail would have had to immediately decide to send his children back to Carlisle right after withdrawing them, which seems unlikely as he was adamantly against what he had witnessed there. During the same visit when Ernest White Thunder had tried to run away, Spotted Tail withdrew all of his children, three of whom—Oliver (Pulls), Pollock (Little Scout), and Max (Talks with Bears)—re-enrolled after his death.[5] His daughter Gertrude (Stands and Laughs) enrolled for the first time in November 1882. Of the four children who returned to Carlisle, three would die there or shortly after being discharged due to illness.

Brenda J. Child has shown how Native American parents often turned to boarding schools to feed and care for their children in times of economic and social crisis. She terms social conditions such as "poverty, diaspora, and disease" that resulted from periods of heightened or ongoing colonial violence the "legacies of dispossession" (Child 1998, 12). Spotted Tail's relatives likely had similar reasons for enrolling the children when their father died unexpectedly and violently after decades of war, ongoing hunger, and political upheaval at the Rosebud Agency. Two of Spotted Tail's children died in 1883—Gertrude on an outing and Oliver after being discharged for ill health. Max was also discharged due to ill health in 1885 and died at Rosebud. Within the context of uncertainty as to the value of an education at Carlisle, Spotted Tail had been a steadfast critic even as other Sicangu leaders like White Thunder embraced Pratt and his project. The deaths of Spotted Tail's children added to the grief and tragedy felt at Rosebud and would result in the complete failure of the Pratt Commission when it came to secure signatures for the Dawes Bill in 1888.

The Dawes Act passed in 1887 and set out to break up reservation lands across the continent into individual allotments, enforcing the norms of private property on Indigenous lands held collectively.[6] The act stipulated that excess tribal lands would be opened to settlement and also determined that any Native American man "who has voluntarily taken up, within said limits, his residence separate and apart from any tribe of Indians therein, and has adopted the habits of civilized life, is hereby declared to be a citizen of the United States" ("An Act to Provide for the Allotment of Lands" n.d.). The act was a judicial version of Pratt's educational work to "Kill the Indian, Save the Man." Both promised the benefits of American citizenship to those Indians who would surrender their land and language to disappear into the American polity. Under the 1868 treaty agreement, the federal government needed three-quarters of the males to consent to implement the act on the Great Sioux Reservation, and Pratt was selected to lead a commission to get the required signatures. The Indian Bureau believed Pratt would be an excellent emissary because of his ongoing relationship with the Lakota and his earlier success in enrolling their children at Carlisle. In fact, Pratt's commission was a complete failure. From Standing Rock to Rosebud, everyone met Pratt with a wall of resistance. They would not consent to breaking apart any of their remaining 22 million acres (Estes 2019, 120). Pratt needed thousands of signatures; he got 120 (Estes 2019, 121).

Why did Pratt fail so spectacularly? He does not mention the Dawes Commission in his memoir, leaving in place his narrative of a triumphant career of good relations with Indians. One clue appears not in his own writings but in those of his successor, George Crook, who wrote to Washington that he was struggling to obtain the required signatures during his own trip to the Dakotas because of unanswered questions about the sickness, deaths, and remains of children at Carlisle. In 1889, Crook wrote to the US Congress that leaders across agencies refused to sign, citing previous unfulfilled promises including "the failure to improve the poor quality of annuity goods such as clothing and farming equipment, and continued unexplained deaths of children at off-reservation boarding schools such as Carlisle" (quoted in Estes 2019, 122). The bodies of Ernest, Maude, and many others appear again as sites of injustice on which the Oceti Sakowin would articulate their resistance. Ultimately, Crook turned to lies and threats to get signatures. He promised that the Dawes Bill would alleviate hardship on reservations without changing existing treaty stipulations. In reality, the bill would greatly reduce the 1868 treaty lands. He also threatened to criminalize Red Cloud and his followers at Pine Ridge if they did not sign (Estes 2019, 122). Through these tactics, Crook managed to divide the resistance Pratt had encountered and obtain the signatures to enforce allotment, opening 9 million acres to settlement. The act became known as the "1889 Sioux Agreement" and created the boundaries for the Pine Ridge, Rosebud, Cheyenne River, Standing Rock, Lower Brule, and Crow Creek Reservations, which remain in place today (Estes 2019, 122).

When Ernest White Thunder engaged in a hunger strike to death, he could not have known what significance his death would ultimately have. But his self-starvation amplified and brought attention to the deaths of other children and how the Carlisle staff responded by making excuses and ignoring demands that the children's remains be sent home. Once the Sicangu saw how their children's deaths were handled, it became impossible for them to continue to believe Pratt's rhetoric of his benevolent intentions for their people. Ernest's peers also directly witnessed his death and would write about it decades later. When Pratt ignored demands that Ernest's remains be sent home, this, too, lived on in the memory of the students, including the famous Lakota historian and memoirist Standing Bear. Ernest's body and the bodies of his peers emerge again and again in the written record, through letters, petitions, memoirs, and histories. Ultimately, Ernest's death by self-starvation forced his captors to reveal their colonial motivations to the Lakota people, who would then continue to resist US claims of benevolence in future negotiations. As one of the earliest rhetors to use a hunger strike to make public the immorality of the powerful who held him captive, Ernest deserves recognition as an important Sicangu leader who invented new means to resist dispossession and tribal erasure.

RETURNED STUDENTS' RHETORICS OF REFUSAL

As the Dawes Act took hold, the Oceti Sakowin found their lands restricted more than ever before. Hunger plagued reservation life as traditional buffalo-hunting practices became impossible, crops failed, and the federal government withheld sufficient annuity goods. At the same time, young people were beginning to return from Carlisle where, despite Pratt's promises, their education had not equipped them to survive in this new order. Students returned to reservation life able to speak English, farm, and practice trades; but their skills were not compatible with the reservation economy. One such returned student, Plenty Horses (Senika-Wakan-Ota), would deploy his own rhetoric of refusal in the years to come, becoming active in the Ghost Dance movement and famously killing US Army lieutenant Edward W. Casey in reprisal for the Wounded Knee Massacre.[7] When Plenty Horses went to trial, he implicated Carlisle in his violent act, using his notoriety to lay bare the damage Carlisle had caused the young people who went to school there. Like Ernest White Thunder, Plenty Horses would place his embodied acts in relation to English-language print to register his resistance. Also like White Thunder, he was willing to die to shore up the future of his nation.

Plenty Horses, the son of Sicangu headman Living Bear, left Rosebud and attended Carlisle from 1883 through 1888, then returned to live at Pine Ridge. He shot Lieutenant Edward Casey on January 7, 1891, eight days after the Wounded Knee Massacre and two years after his return from school. During his grand jury testimony, he said "[For] five years I attended Carlisle and was educated in the ways of the white man. When I returned to my people, I was an outcast among them. I was no longer an Indian. I was not a white man. I was lonely . . . I shot the lieutenant so I might make a place for myself among my people. I am now one of them. I shall be hung, and the Indians will bury me as a warrior" (quoted in Fear-Segal and Rose 2016, 3).[8] Like Ernest White Thunder, Plenty Horses disarms the fantasy of benevolence under which Pratt and the Friends of the Indian operated. He blames Carlisle for his crisis of identity. He further implicates his education in the ongoing violence between the Lakota and the United States. Carlisle was supposed to solve the "Indian Problem," but Plenty Horses shows that the school is just another site in the ongoing war between the Lakota and the United States. Also like Ernest, he sees his death as a way to reclaim his national identity. In his testimony he deploys the figure of his hanging body to refuse the assimilationist narrative Pratt and the off-reservation boarding school movement are propagating. Through a brave death, Plenty Horses hopes to join his nation and erase the education he experienced. He chooses death over assimilation.

Carlisle played a crucial role in Plenty Horses's murder trial. When his defense attorneys called him to the stand, the prosecuting attorney insisted that Plenty Horses testify in English. All of the other Indian witnesses had been able to testify in their own languages with translations provided by interpreter Philip Wells, but the judges agreed that Plenty

Horses had to testify in English because of his education at Carlisle. This led his defense attorneys to keep him off the stand (Utley 1974). Carlisle promised the benefits of citizenship to all students who attended and insisted that an English-only, assimilationist education would ultimately give them a better life. Instead, English became a tool of cultural genocide within the school and beyond its walls. During the trial, Plenty Horses's English literacy was used to strip him of his rhetorical sovereignty. He did not want to tell his story in the language of his enemies, a language he stopped using as soon as he returned to Pine Ridge. In an interview during his trial with reporter John A. McDonough of the *New York World*, Plenty Horses said:

> I found that the education I had received was of no benefit to me. There was no chance to get employment, nothing for me to do whereby I could earn my board and clothes, no opportunity to learn more and remain with the whites. It disheartened me and I went back to live as I had before going to school. To forget my school habits and English speech was an easy matter. (quoted in Utley 1974)

In his public speech surrounding the trial, Plenty Horses discussed the ways Carlisle failed him. Plenty Horses laid bare how Pratt failed to fulfill his promises. Industrial training and English literacy would not help the Lakota as long as the US government persisted in its ongoing attempts to dispossess them. Plenty Horses publicly rejected his cultural training as well, no longer speaking English or dressing in Euro-American attire. He grew out his hair and wore it in braids. He fashioned himself as the opposite of the model students Pratt publicized in his before-and-after photos and newspaper editorials. He refused everything he had learned at Carlisle and made his refusal a crucial part of his public narrative in the periodical press. His body and testimony appeared in periodicals as an argument against everything Pratt stood for.

Ultimately, Plenty Horses was not convicted because his defense attorneys argued successfully that he had killed Casey under conditions of war; therefore, the murder could not be a crime. Plenty Horses went free because if he was guilty of murder, so, too, were the soldiers who massacred men, women, and children at Wounded Knee Creek. Although Plenty Horses did not have to die to communicate his membership in his nation or erase his years at Carlisle, he drew on the same repertoire as many other Sicangu rhetors. He refused to become a civilized Indian and in so doing revealed the violence behind the promise of assimilationist education.

In 1901—ten years after Plenty Horses's acquittal—Dakota author and former Carlisle teacher Zitkála-Šá published a story called "The

Soft Hearted Sioux" in *Harper's Monthly Magazine* (2003c). Her fictional account resonates strongly with Plenty Horses's story and shows how the embodied acts of Plenty Horses, like Ernest White Thunder before him, resonated in the imaginations and stories of his people to inspire future acts of resistance in new and emerging publics. Ernest White Thunder, Luther Standing Bear, and Plenty Horses were all in the first group of students sent to Carlisle. Zitkála-Šá entered an off-reservation boarding school in Indiana a few years later, in 1884. At age eight, she left the Yankton Reservation, an experience she writes about in her autobiographical essays *The School Days of an Indian Girl* (2003b). In 1897, she became a full-time teacher at Carlisle. These experiences led her to write scathing critiques of Pratt, Carlisle, and the boarding school movement as a whole, which had become compulsory in the United States by 1891. Her story of the agonizing ordeal of a returned student demonstrates how Lakota embodied rhetorics resonated into the twentieth century as returned students found new ways to push back against assimilationist education.

The protagonist of "The Soft Hearted Sioux" spends nearly a decade away from his family at a missionary school learning to speak English and preach the Christian faith. He shares some aspects of Plenty Horses's story—he can still speak his own language when he returns, his father is a famous warrior in his nation, and he eventually shoots a white man because of the desperate position of his liminal cultural identity. He also narrates his tale from a jail cell to an unnamed listener, much as Plenty Horses tells his story to journalists during his trial. Most important, the soft-hearted Sioux believes his death by hanging will solidify his cultural identity once and for all. His language mirrors the value of a brave death in Lakota culture as articulated by Ernest White Thunder, Luther Standing Bear, and Plenty Horses. On the morning before his execution, he thinks "my hands hang quietly at my side. Serene and brave, my soul awaits the men to perch me on the gallows for another flight. I go" (Zitkála-Šá 2003c, 126).

But this is where the similarities end. Unlike Plenty Horses, the narrator has fully embraced boarding school teachings, especially Christianity. His characterization indicts not only the boarding school movement but also the longer history of Christian missionaries who disguise colonization as salvation. When the narrator returns to the reservation to find his father is very ill, he stops a medicine man from treating his father and refuses to hunt to feed his family. He believes these practices are barbaric and un-Christian. When the community abandons the narrator for being a traitor, he slaughters a settler's cow and steals the meat, then kills the white man who pursues him for the theft. When he returns home, his father has died of starvation. The narrator then turns himself in to the authorities to be tried and hanged for murder. This character is a tragic Indian, the kind of figure Gerald Vizenor (1994) critiques as a colonial creation. But the tragedy here is not his Indigenous culture but rather his adoption of settler culture. By accepting the orthodoxy of the Christian missionaries and the boarding school movement, he destroys himself, his family, and his nation. Zitkála-Šá reframes the Carlisle motto—rather than killing the Indian to save the man, she shows how the school's true mission is to kill the Indian, full stop. There is no salvation or redemption for the returned students. The boarding school movement is revealed for what it is—education for dispossession.

Zitkála-Šá draws another connection between Carlisle and her tragic narrator through his name. Changing students' names was one of the earliest ways the Carlisle teachers implemented their assimilationist methods. Recalling Luther Standing Bear's memory of his first days at Carlisle, the teachers often replaced students' names with those of famous Euro-Americans such as Abe Lincoln or Rutherford B. Hayes. This is how Wica-karpa became Ernest White Thunder, an arbitrary English first name combined with the name of Ernest's father. Plenty Horses's Carlisle name was Plenty Living Bear. By renaming the children, the teachers ensured that their names would fit within Western norms of patrilineal descent to enable the shift to individual property ownership and inheritance. The cultural position of the returned students is brought into stark relief through the tension around their names, and Zitkála-Šá makes naming one of the central ambiguities of her narrative of the "Soft Hearted Sioux." As the tale begins, we learn that the narrator has not yet won a title by proving himself as a hunter and warrior (Zitkála-Šá 2003c, 118). When he returns from boarding school, we do not find out what his Americanized name is. "Soft-Hearted Sioux" thus becomes his only name, an ironic and pejorative title. Because he missed his opportunity to gain a Lakota name, this title highlights his distance from his nation, not his belonging within it.

Zitkála-Šá, too, has a fraught relationship with naming. Born Gertrude Simmons, she chose her Lakota name Zitkála-Šá or Red Bird when she returned to Pine Ridge in 1901. Her sister-in-law told her not to use her brother's last name—Bonnin—because she had abandoned her family to get an education. In a letter to her fiancé Carlos Montezuma, Zitkála-Šá wrote "well—you can guess how queer I felt—away from my own people—homeless—penniless—and even without a name! Then I chose to make a name for myself—and I guess

I have made 'Zitkála-Šá' known" (quoted in Bernardin 1997, 230). Here the term *queer* highlights her alienation from her national identity and how refusing her English name was an attempt to alleviate that alienation. She also suggests that by making her Lakota name known in the periodical press, she is working to recover her national identity through a critique of her colonial education. Mark Rifkin's (2006, 45) reading of *American Indian Stories, Legends, and Other Writings* (Zitkála-Šá 2003a) argues that one way Zitkála-Šá's writing can be seen as queer is through her attempt to "make traditional native social formations and modes of self-representation intelligible to white readers." I would add that when Zitkála-Šá acknowledges the queer positionality of a returned student, she critiques the violence of colonial education. As a returned student like Plenty Horses, she uses the print public sphere to make sense of her experiences in boarding schools and to refuse the legacy of her assimilationist education. Zitkála-Šá (2003a, 113) comes to wonder if "real life or long-lasting death lies beneath the semblance of civilization." She uses her boarding school experience to give voice to boarding school students in the print public sphere of the United States. By doing so, she creates new relations between alphabetic literacy and Indigenous stories in the Assimilation Era, using the very technology that was forced upon her to question the legitimacy of settler society.

When Richard Henry Pratt convinced the Sicangu Oyate to send their children to Carlisle, he promised that the school would help their people survive and defend their territory. As the first students at Carlisle, these young people discovered that Pratt's benevolence was a fiction, and they began a decades-long process of inventing ways to refuse assimilationist education. Ernest White Thunder was the first Sicangu boy to communicate his absolute refusal to engage with the English-only project through his embodied acts. His death made clear that Carlisle was not a place of Indigenous futurity but an institution designed to bring about the end of Indigenous cultures. Ernest's embodied resistance cleared the way for multiple forms of Sicangu refusal that appeared in oral, print, and literary media, from Spotted Tail's x-mark to Plenty Horses's trial testimony. These refusals generated new forms of expression as bodily acts entered print to indict the boarding school movement. Lakota rhetorics of refusal inspired ongoing and generative new means of survivance for the Oceti Sakowin in one of the most violent periods of colonization in the history of the confederacy.

4
WRITING THEIR BODIES IN THE PERIODICAL PRESS

Carlisle students learned to communicate and to shape their worlds within and against forces of war, assimilation, and allotment. Prior to coming to school, these young people lived their entire lives in violent conflict with the US military. They viewed Euro-Americans as their enemies. Almost all of the first children at Carlisle were related to tribal leaders. They were the children of men and women who had most strongly resisted the US government after the Civil War. Chiefs Joseph, Spotted Tail, Red Cloud, and Geronimo all sent children to Carlisle. Some were incarcerated and saw no other way for their children to get enough food. Others believed that learning English would give their children a better chance to resist increasing pressure from settlers and the US government. The government demanded that Richard Henry Pratt take the children of detained prisoners of war and hostile bands. It was in the US military interest to bring these young people to central Pennsylvania—far from their parents, their languages, and their homelands.

In the Carlisle periodical press, this context is easy to miss. As a result, much writing from the boarding school period has been dismissed as transparently assimilationist. There are other constraints that make these students' rhetorical situation difficult to fully grasp. Students are referred to by their English names, so we cannot easily understand where they came from, who their families were, or the desperate conditions that influenced their parents to send them to school. Sometimes they are anonymous, such as the Nez Perce girl whose writing I examine in this chapter. In addition, their words and messages are always coerced. Everywhere in this archive are compositions from classes on the topic of why Euro-American culture is superior to Indian cultures. Students' writing falls under other forms of surveillance and coercion as well. All letters are read by Pratt and his staff. There is no private written communication. And so, these children who have lived through war their entire lives are suddenly championing their enemies and all they stand for. The written record is not enough to understand who these

DOI: 10.7330/9781646420872.c004

children were or how they used language to negotiate their captivity at school. A rhetoric of relations ameliorates this interpretive problem. By reading other forms of media, a rhetoric of relations demands that we credit these young people with strategic acts of survivance.

If students were so limited in what they could say—punished for speaking in their own language, humiliated for making mistakes—they were even more limited in what they could write. What was left? The infinite communicative repository of the body. In her study of disability and Native North American boarding school narratives, Penelope Kelsey (2013, 199) argues that "boarding school narrators' reflections on their experiences at home and at school, their cultures and languages of origin, and their bodies remain unexamined as sites of Indigenous knowledge formation." While Kelsey is looking at later reflections on boarding school experiences, my interest is in how students' narratives of their bodies entered their texts while they were at school. I argue that students used their bodies to circulate meaning among their peers, with their distant families, and with the Euro-American readers of their texts. Students wrote stories of their bodies into letters and newspapers to communicate the cruel conditions of their lives under settler supervision and control. If we recognize the embodied rhetorics of Carlisle students, we can see how these young people metabolized their assimilationist training and turned it into unexpected and unruly acts of survivance.

THE PERIODICAL PRESS AND THE CIVILIZATIONAL PROJECT

The periodical played a number of important roles at Carlisle, many of which have been explored at length in the existing scholarship. Historian David Wallace Adams (1995) draws much of his research from materials in the periodical record, showing how the Carlisle newspapers captured and disseminated the school's assimilationist views and methods. Jessica Enoch (2008, 74) has noted that "these publications proudly informed supporters of Indian education of the ways Carlisle's teachers were successfully 'civilizing' Indian 'savages' by transforming them into self-sufficient individuals." And Amelia Katanski (2005, 44) has demonstrated how Pratt and his staff used periodicals to produce evidence of their success by controlling representations of students and "by sanctioning or producing only representations of total transformation." But how is it that the periodical quickly became such a central aspect of a school purportedly teaching all kinds of trades, from tinsmithing to military discipline, that on their face have little to do with print media? The answer lies in the interlocking processes of nation building, education, and periodical print culture in the nineteenth century.

As Pratt worked to civilize his students, he drew on nineteenth-century beliefs about the power of technological advancement to justify the imperial activities of the United States. As the nation expanded, settlers made use of the telegraph, the railroad, and the cylinder press to both facilitate settlement of the West and imagine themselves as more advanced and adaptable than the Indians whose land they were appropriating. Periodical print culture shifted quickly due to massive changes in the availability of printed materials and literate audiences between 1820 and 1850, and the increase in periodical publications became inextricable from national efforts to make literacy education available to a broadening group of citizens. In 1825, there were approximately 100 periodicals in circulation, but by 1840, that number had increased to 1,500. Kenneth M. Price and Susan Belasco Smith (1995, 3–5) attribute this expansion to advancements in papermaking, the widespread availability of the cylinder press, cheaper postal routes, rising literacy rates brought about by common schools,[1] and widespread distribution by railroad. Carl F. Kaestle (1991, 65) has identified "a reciprocal relationship between literacy and publication." As more Americans learned to read, they created a larger market for printed materials, which, in turn, facilitated the increase in the number of literate Americans. The periodical press and national education were so intertwined that Margaret Fuller wrote in 1852 that "the most important part of our literature, while the work of diffusion is still going on, lies in the journals, which monthly, weekly, daily, send their messages to every corner of this great land, and form at present, the only efficient instrument for the general education of the people" (quoted in Price and Belasco Smith 1995, 6). As the United States expanded, print technologies became the most ubiquitous modes of education for the dispersed population.

Margaret Fuller's vision of the periodical disseminated over "every corner of this great land" resonates with Benedict Anderson's formulation of the nation as an imagined community tied together by print capitalism. For Fuller and her contemporary nineteenth-century Euro-Americans, the boundaries of the nation were determined by how far its print public sphere extended across geographic space. Anderson theorizes the periodical as a means of national cohesion. He argues that the reading of newspapers is a national ceremony: "It is performed in silent privacy, in the lair of the skull. Yet each communicant is well aware that the ceremony he performs is being replicated simultaneously by thousands (or millions) of others of whose existence he is confident, yet of whose identity he has not the slightest notion" (Anderson 1991, 35). For Anderson (1991, 7), the imagined "deep, horizontal comradeship" of the nation becomes tangible when a reader sees others around her reading the same papers. Although audiences will never know the majority of their national cohorts, they develop a sense of one another as shared cultural practitioners through periodical reading. Pratt had a very similar vision for his periodicals. Not only would they inform his benefactors of the successful work being done at Carlisle, but returned students would form an imagined community, maintaining their cultural kinship with Euro-Americans as they returned to far-flung reservations by reading the *Red Man* and the *Indian Helper*, two later iterations of the *Eadle Keatah Toh.*

Richard Brodhead's concept of the domestic/tutelary complex is also helpful to make sense of why Pratt placed so much value on the school periodicals. Like Fuller, Brodhead argues that periodical reading in the home was the primary mode of education in an expanding nation. For Broadhead, children internalize the discipline and industry that will make them good Protestant workers through their domestic reading practices. They do their learning, ideally, in a loving family home where reading is the principal pedagogical and social activity (Brodhead 1993, 45). As Carlisle students were ripped away from their homes and placed in boarding schools, we can imagine that the Carlisle reading room became just such a pedagogical space for the development of discipline, industry, and a sense of belonging in the United States.

Carlisle printed its first paper, the *Eadle Keatah Toh*, in January 1880, a few months after the first students arrived. Periodicals worked in concert with the before-and-after photographs to communicate the cultural transformations Pratt wanted to demonstrate to the public and his funders. For this reason, Pratt often used student writing as a mouthpiece for his own views. The Carlisle periodicals also served as disciplinary and surveillance devices (82). Students were publicly named and shamed for language errors or for speaking in their own languages. Classroom compositions were reprinted to demonstrate exemplary students' work, and students were mentioned by name if they were not learning as quickly as their teachers thought they should be or if they were not sufficiently obedient to school rules and regulations.

The periodicals facilitated both industrial and English-literacy training. Native apprentices set the type for all publications and edited their own amateur newspaper, the *School News*. This paper was available at the school for students to read, and anyone around the country could subscribe. It ran from June 1880 through May 1883 with one four-page volume per month, during what was almost exactly the first three-year term of students at Carlisle. Printing was one of the trades among many such as tinsmithing, farming, and blacksmithing that made up the industrial component of the curriculum. The *School News*, then, is a rich site to explore the compositions of Native students, as they contributed content, set type, and edited the final product. Yet as Katanski (2005, 83) has argued, the student texts in this and other papers were "closely controlled, and very aware of being watched and judged." The amateur newspaper shows what kinds of writing students engaged in but also demonstrates the assimilationist rhetoric Pratt and his contemporaries crafted and then imposed on student writers.

This amateur newspaper can tell us much about the relationship between industrial and literacy training at Carlisle in its early years, as well as how students interpreted, responded to, and challenged their English-only education. Kathleen Washburn (2012, 380) has noted increased scholarly attention to the Indigenous archive. She looks at the publications of the Society of American Indians, a "vexed addition to expanding Indigenous archives because of the group's association with the national project of assimilating Indigenous people to a rigid domestic order in the early twentieth century" (381). The *School News* offers a similar challenge to a reader looking for a resistant narrative of Indigenous expression. Neither obedient nor entirely defiant, the contents of this paper demand new modes for making sense of Native voices. This chapter offers some ways we might think through the experience of Native students learning to read, write, and speak English by reading for their relational rhetorics in seemingly obedient texts. The *School News* demands careful and contextualized reading practices that take seriously Native rhetorical dispositions within and beyond alphabetic text.

The amateur newspaper emerged as a popular children's literacy training tool in the second half of the nineteenth century. Like hundreds of middle-class Euro-American children around the United States, Carlisle students produced a newspaper of four pages, 8 inches by 11 inches or smaller, published once a month (Schultz 1999, 136). The *School News* took part in the peak of the medium's popularity. In 1867, Benjamin O. Woods invented a novelty press that cost only a few dollars and became a popular household item in the 1870s and 1880s. While the *School News* was likely printed on the same press as the professional paper at Carlisle and not on Woods's novelty press, Pratt and his teachers were certainly aware of the popularity of amateur papers and would likely have suggested that their students take part in the genre as part of their exposure to Euro-American culture. At least 5,500 known amateur newspapers were published throughout the United States in the nineteenth century.[2] The town of Carlisle had its own amateur newspaper, titled *Everybody's Hand-Book*, in addition to the *School News* between January and May 1877. Written by Euro-American Carlisle children, this newspaper contained recipes for various home remedies and foods as well as excerpted stories and poems and a puzzle section. The *School News* was markedly less playful. Used as a teaching, surveillance, and assimilationist tool, the amateur newspaper at the Carlisle school gives us a lens into how Pratt thought his students should be interacting with literacy and how they made that literacy their own by writing about their subtle embodied experiences alongside more explicit stories of their enthusiastic embracing of the Carlisle project.

Lucille Schultz (1999, 108) terms the practices of nineteenth-century student composers such as letters, diaries, newspapers, and memoirs the "extracurriculum" and urges us "to listen to the voices of the young composers: the receivers rather than the deliverers of instruction, the authors of texts that to date have received the least attention from composition historians." For Schultz (1999, 134), the extracurriculum is a "site for self-expression and for resistance that was not ordinarily available in classroom-based writing." Forced letter and periodical writing at Carlisle complicate this rosy portrayal, perhaps even illustrating a tendency in rhetoric and composition that Malea Powell (2002, 398) has identified as "deliberately unseeing its participation in imperialism." If we contextualize the extracurriculum in light of English-only training, we would have to reckon with how composition history is imperial history. There is simply no way to laud the resistant, expressive letters and periodicals of nineteenth-century children without acknowledging how these genres perpetrated cultural violence for young composers outside of white middle-class households.

The *School News* appears at the intersection of multiple innovations in periodical print culture that took place over the course of the nineteenth century. Because it is designed to bring Indian children into the national fold, we can understand it alongside not only the other Carlisle periodicals but also the landscape of periodical print culture in nineteenth-century America. The *School News* can also be understood as an example of Indigenous cultures of print in the nineteenth century,[3] as part of the ongoing effort by Indigenous nations to strengthen their political and social positions in opposition to settler-colonial incursions and racialist beliefs about the deficits of Native American culture.

Finally, the *School News* shows how writing pedagogy, from diaries to letters to amateur newspapers, is not made up of neutral or benevolent genres for young people but rather is the means through which settler educators sought to destroy and replace Indigenous communicative practices and rhetorical modes. The remainder of the chapter will look at two students' writing to see how they engaged the space of the amateur newspaper, what they wrote, and how they wrote about their bodies to materialize their resistance in ways that would have been illegible to their teachers.

CHARLES KIHEGA'S VISIT HOME

In August 1881, Samuel Townsend turned over editorship of the *School News* to Charles Kihega. Samuel had been editing the publication since its first issue in June 1880. Charles, or Charlie, came to Carlisle shortly after the first Lakota children, arriving in late February 1880 at age eighteen.[4] He began working in the printer's office in October of that year[5] and was likely assigned to this trade because he had previous experience with English from having attended a mission school in Nebraska.[6] Given his responsibility of editing the amateur paper as well as setting type for the *Eadle Keatah Toh*, we can tell that Charles was one of the most advanced English speakers and writers among Carlisle's first students. He spent the summer of 1882 at home with his family and two letters from that visit appear in his paper, one year into his editorship. These letters exhibit the perspective of a student who has embraced English literacy and then returns home to put his education to use.

The summer of 1882 was a time of transition for Carlisle. The Lakota students had reached their agreed-upon three-year term, and most decided to return home to Rosebud and Pine Ridge on June 19. Both the student newspaper and the *Eadle Keatah Toh* began to register the administration's anxiety about how the students would maintain their cultural training at home. The administration was also concerned about how the school would return to an English-only environment with the most experienced students gone and an influx of new students entering in the fall. At the same time, Charles Kihega took a break from his duties as editor of the *School News* and typesetter for the *Eadle Keatah Toh* to visit his family for three months in White Cloud, Kansas.

Charles wrote to Carlisle in August of that summer, and his letter appears in vol. 3, no. 4 of the *School News*. He had been away from his home and the Ioway people for two years and five months, and the visit was fraught with expectations and disappointments. Charles was an

Figure 4.1. Studio portrait of Richard Pratt's son, Mason Pratt (seated at left), Charles Kihega (standing), Samuel Townsend (seated at right), and Benjamin Marshall (Creek Nation) (seated in center). Photo by John N. Choate, ca. 1882. Courtesy, Cumberland County Historical Society, Carlisle, PA.

important test case for Pratt's curriculum—here was a student who had excelled not only in the English language but in writing, editing, and the printer trade as well. Even so, I imagine that Pratt and his colleagues were anxious that Kihega might not come back to school after his visit. Charles, too, must have wondered how his family would react to the changes he had gone through during his time in the East. Like Ernest White Thunder, Charles Kihega's rhetoric was situated within forces far beyond his individual agency. Hoping to maintain his position of literate authority at the school while demonstrating his pride as an Ioway,

Charles wrote to reconcile his competing identities and show what a returned student could do with his education in support of his nation. He wrote to understand his new relations to his home and nation after embracing the process of learning English at school.

Charles's letter[7] illustrates how he engages with Euro-American culture when he leaves school. He emphasizes timeliness and industry throughout by detailing the trains he took and writing that he "had everything ready before bed" so he could take an early morning train from Atchison, Kansas, to White Cloud. This was a common practice at Carlisle when students traveled to Washington, DC, or Philadelphia. Charles must have learned to organize travel in this way from his experience at school. David Wallace Adams (1995, 117) has identified the "relentless regimentation" of boarding school life, which taught students to organize their time on strict schedules, breaking down the day with "a seemingly endless number of bugles and bells demanding this or that response." Charles shows that he can replicate this temporal system. He goes on at length about what trains he took and when, as well as how he prepared his belongings at night so he would be on time the next day. When he writes "I had no trouble to come up here," Charles is showing that he understands the technological and temporal worldview of Euro-American culture. He can easily navigate the newly regimented landscape of his homeland.

Charles also takes care to emphasize how his family and the Ioway people are hard workers and effective farmers. He does not find his "folks at home," he writes, "because they were out in the field working." He says, "The Iowas have raised good crops this year. They have wheat just as good as any white farmers have." Charles shows pride that his community can produce wheat as well as white farmers can and shows his peers and teachers at Carlisle that his tribe is successful. He emphasizes his own continued industriousness as well. He reports that he worked for two-and-a-half days at home and then went to his aunt's farm when his father ran out of work for him to do. He even translates that labor into currency, calculating "if I came home to stay I could earn thirty dollars a month." Charles shows his teachers that he works hard without Pratt's supervision and that his tribe, too, participates in industriousness. Charles disavows the myth of the lazy Indian that he has been taught at school. The pride he feels as an Ioway indicates that he has maintained a sense of tribal identity after two-and-a-half years away.

In spite of his hard work and sense of pride, all is not well. Charles says he neglected to write home to tell his family he was coming, so no one met him at the train station. And even though he has "plenty of milk to drink," Charles says "I do not feel well since I came home. I feel funny all the time." In these statements, Charles uses his body to register a complaint. He may have expected a joyful homecoming, but his distance from family and community has made his home foreign and uncomfortable. Even as Charles attempts to model the ideal returned student, he hints that the process of reintegration is painful and maybe impossible after so much time. Charles is in a particularly difficult position because he spent so much time setting the type for Pratt's newspapers and replicating assimilationist ideology in his own editorials for the *School News*. The mention of milk, a product of Euro-American agricultural practices imposed on or incorporated by the Ioway, symbolizes all that has changed on the land and indicates that whiteness is making him sick.

After the summer, Charles returned to Carlisle. He resumed editorial duties and included an essay[8] on his visit home in the September volume of the *School News*. Now he tells a different story about his trip home, exclaiming "they were all glad to see me because I had been away from home for two years and five months." In the next lines he reiterates, "I visited all my friends. They have made great improvements in the two years and five months I have been away." While Charles continues to emphasize the progress his community has made, he also repeats the time he has been away. The two years and five months are imprinted on his thoughts as the precise gap between himself and his nation, a gap his visit failed to close.

In this composition, Charles focuses on the geographical schema of Euro-American culture rather than its temporality. He writes, "Every Indian man has a house and from 15–160 acres of good ground fenced in with wire so the cattle and horses can't break in and destroy their crops." Charles speaks here of the geography of allotment, an uneven process that would not take full effect on reservations land until the Dawes Act. It is clear that the Ioway have taken steps to divide their communal lands into individual plots marked by fences and measured acreage. Adams (1995, 113) describes these spatial markers as "a world of lines, corners, and squares," which many students first experienced upon coming to the school. When Charles writes about the success of the Ioway, he demonstrates that success by noting the marked space on which his tribe now lives. He closes his editorial with an echo of Pratt's assimilationist rhetoric: "If the Iowa tribe can learn to farm and take care of themselves I think others can learn [to do the same]." Charles has learned what it means to act white at school, and his tribe has taken on the geography of whiteness at home. The editorial lacks the dissonance of his letter. Now that Charles is back, he uses writing to show how his identity is coherent—he and his people are successful Indians. The Ioway are proficient in marking the land within Euro-American systems of signification. In parallel, Charles is proficient in marking the print public sphere with his English words and printer's type.

Charles's letters demonstrate his struggle to reintegrate with his nation during a long visit home. But there is a larger backdrop of Ioway land disputes that further illuminates his concerns as a member of the Ioway people even as he lived and wrote at school. In February 1882, the winter before Charles visited home, Agent Augustus Brosius at the Great Nemaha Agency wrote to Pratt:

> There is a prospect of a delegation of Indians going from this reserve to Washington to consult with the Indian Dept. in reference to their future, and a portion of the delegation will advocate a removal to the Indian Territory. We think more than half of the tribe desire [*sic*] is remain here and receive their lands as their future homes. Our boys who are at the Carlisle school of course feel interested in the result of this consultation and Charley Kihega, a son of one of the Chiefs has expressed a desire to accompany the delegation and use his influence towards remaining in Nebraska. (Letter from Augustus Brosius to Richard Henry Pratt, February 24, 1882)

In this letter, we can see that one of the main reasons parents and especially leaders decided to send their children to Carlisle was to help them develop English-language literacy so they could advocate for their nations in treaty negotiations and land disputes such as this one. Brosius goes on to say that "Chief Kihega considers his son better qualified to judge in this case than himself and the influence exercised by his presence may be potent for good." Charles has been at school for two years at this point, and his father is calling on him to live up to his promise to help his nation. There is an issue of funds, and Brosius asks if Carlisle can pay for Charles's travel to Washington. While it is unlikely that Charles was able to go to Washington,[9] he did write on the question of his nation's territory in the *School News* that February.

The question under debate was whether the 222 remaining members of the Ioway should remain on their current reservation lands at the Great Nemaha Agency on the Kansas-Nebraska border or relocate to Indian Territory in Oklahoma. The Ioway had been systematically removed from their ancestral lands in Iowa and Missouri over the previous century, and those who wanted to move to Indian Territory were concerned that white settlers would continue to encroach on their current lands. Charles believed the Ioway should stay in Nebraska, writing:

> Half of the tribe packed up their things and went to Indian Territory two or three years ago. They were afraid of the white people. They said, "The

white people [are] all around us; we are in a pen; after [a] while they
will drive us out of our place, and we would starve to death." So they ask
the agent to sell out; but the other half said, "We will not sell out; we will
stay here." So they separated the tribe. They started without permission.
Nobody ever know [*sic*] where they are. I guess, wherever they are, they
camp from place to place to this day. The best thing they could do would
be to go back to Nebraska and stay there as the other half did. Those who
are at home don't care if they are in a "pen," fenced in by white people.
They look ahead and send their children to school. (Kihega 1882b, 2)

For Charles, school is a way to build the future of the Ioway people. His
editorial argues for a middle path moving forward—assimilation in some
areas can keep his people together and thriving on territory that is good
for farming. The language of a "pen" refers to the move to allot land,
or create separate tracts for each family. It resonates also with the pen
as a writing tool. Just as his nation can accept being penned in by white
people on their land, so, too, can Charles accept being penned in by the
English literacy he is practicing at school. For Charles, these compro-
mises are necessary if his nation is to survive the Assimilation Era.

Charles expresses the fact that those who left Nebraska did so to
maintain communal land ownership and continue to practice the old
ways where they "camp from place to place." But there is no guarantee
that land in Indian country will be better for farming or that the US
government won't take that land away one day as well. For Charles, this
uncertainty is no way to proceed into the future. He encourages his people to "look ahead and send their children to school." We can see Pratt's
influence in this editorial, but Charles has a strong voice as well. He is
not arguing that the Ioway should disappear into Euro-American society
but rather engaging in the debate within his nation about the best path
forward for his people. Charles clearly believes Ioway survival will come
from agriculture, schooling, and holding on to their lands in Nebraska
and Kansas. He uses his position as editor of a school paper and writer
to make his case, and I can imagine him making sure his father has
this issue of the *School News* with him when he travels to Washington for
the negotiation.

Charles's writings in the *School News* tell a complicated story about a
young person who came to Carlisle to ensure the survival of his nation.
His writings engage the crucial question facing the Ioway—should they
accede to the demands of the federal government in order to stay on
their prosperous lands in Kansas and Nebraska, or should they remove
again to Indian Territory in hopes of regaining some of their traditional
subsistence practices and avoiding the allotment and educational policies being forced on them? When he writes "I do not feel well since I

came home. I feel funny all the time," he is articulating an embodied response to the stress pursuing his education has caused him. He has lost his sense of belonging in his nation. And yet, he clearly articulates that he makes this choice to secure Ioway survivance in the face of an uncertain future. Ultimately, the Ioway Nation split in two, with those remaining in Kansas losing significant landholdings to allotment in 1887 and those in Oklahoma gaining a reservation by Executive Order in 1883 but losing most of their territory to allotment and the Oklahoma land rush of 1891.[10] In the face of inescapable colonial power, Charles used his hard-won English literacy to argue for Ioway presence on their land into the next century. He negotiated his new relations with his nation and the Ioway's shifting relations with a rapacious colonial enemy through writing.

THE DISSONANT RHETORIC OF A STUDENT ON OUTING

The *School News* captures the experiences of the first off-reservation boarding school students. It is also a medium through which they negotiated their changing relations to nation, land, and language. The letter is another medium through which students made meaning of their changing social relations. Letter writing was an important part of the Carlisle literacy curriculum. Students had to write at least one letter to their families in English each month. Pratt hoped the students would adopt letter writing as a Euro-American literacy practice. They were also required to write in diaries and read periodicals such as the *Eadle Keatah Toh* and the *School News*. Often, these media overlapped. Carlisle periodicals regularly reprinted passages from students' diaries and their letters home, which, in turn, became reading material for the other students. This process is the beginning of what Amanda Zink has called "Carlisle's Writing Circle." In her study of how the Carlisle writing curriculum impacted Native women writers, she suggests that "once taught to write . . . Indian girls became women writers who shaped their own responses to their domestic education and would manipulate the sentimental discourse in ways reformers and officials could have never predicted and would have never desired" (Zink 2015, 39). Robert Warrior (2005, 1000) has also pointed to Native students' boarding school writing as a cornerstone in the development of a Native American literary tradition, referring to "Native educational texts as a microcosm of Native literary history."

To conclude this chapter, I call our attention to the writing life of a Nez Perce girl named Harriet Mary Elder who learned to write at Carlisle and then repurposed Euro-American literacy practices such

Figure 4.2. Studio portrait of Alice Wynn (Sioux Nation) (back left), Kisetta Roosevelt (Apache Lipan Nation) (back middle), Mabel Doanmoe (Kiowa Nation) (back right), Rebecca Big Star (Sioux Nation) (front left), and Harriet Mary Elder (Nez Perce Nation) (front right). Photo by John N. Choate, March 1880. Courtesy, Cumberland County Historical Society, Carlisle, PA.

as letter writing and periodical print to make sense of her gendered experience of assimilationist policies. Harriet Mary is in many ways the opposite of a writer like Zitkála-Šá. She never explicitly rejects her boarding school education but rather uses that education to make a place for herself as a Nez Perce woman in a rapidly changing social environment. Yet like Zitkála-Šá, Harriet Mary Elder learned to write at boarding school and continued to publish in periodicals after she went to live on the Nez Perce Reservation in Idaho. This student exemplifies what it meant to survive by performing assimilation in her writing. Her writings illuminate the violence, chaos, and identity loss Carlisle students faced and how even the most seemingly obedient texts carry within them stories of students using English literacy to push back against the injustices of their educational experiences.

Harriet Mary's first known writing emerges from the same fraught period in Carlisle's early history as Charles Kihega's letter from home. In the summer of 1882, students came close to the end of their three-year terms, and Pratt began the next phase of his educational program—outing students on local farms. Pratt developed his "outing program" with Samuel Chapman Armstrong at Hampton. Both believed that placing children who had working proficiency in English on farms under the supervision of rural Euro-American families would help reduce prejudice and build understanding between American citizens and "noncitizen Indians" (Pratt 1964, 312). In practice, outing became a source of free labor for Pennsylvania farmers and a radical assimilationist experience for Native children. These students still wrote letters, but now they wrote to the Carlisle administration and staff instead of to their families. Through this shift in the audience of their letters, students began to write about Carlisle as a second home for which they learned to express nostalgia. The outing program worked as yet another relocation from Indigenous identity as students had to rebuild affective and kinship connections for a second time since coming to the school. One month after his return from Kansas, in the October 1882 edition of the *School News*, Charles Kihega includes a "a letter from a Nez Perce, in school two years and a half," who has gone on outing. In the letter,[11] Harriet Mary's name is not included, and I expand on the importance of that omission in what follows.

This letter demonstrates some of the dissonance that emerges when a young girl writes to surrogate parental figures at Carlisle. She addresses the letter "Dear School Father, Miss Ely or Captain Pratt," articulating how these authority figures have supplanted her parents as primary kinship ties. Her first line asks "I would like to know if the Captain is home now," revealing that Carlisle has become a home for her over the past two-and-a-half years. Harriet Mary later says she hopes "all of the school daughters and the teachers and youself [*sic*] are getting along nicely," characterizing herself and her peers as "daughters" of the teacher-parents. This familial language brings to light the insidious ways government schools tried to break up the Indian family, as Beth Piatote (2013, 5) has argued, in an effort "to cultivate children's allegiance to the United States rather than to the tribe." Mark Rifkin (2006, 28) has also identified Carlisle's gendered curriculum as part of "a network of interlocking state-sanctioned policies and ideologies that positioned monogamous hetero couple hood and the privatized single-family household as official national ideals." Gender training and family replacement were part of the larger project of detribalization and allotment wherein single-family units replaced tribal kinship structures and a domestic division of labor mirrored the imagined ideal of the Euro-American yeoman home. Pratt has aimed to create a parent-child dynamic with his students, so it is no surprise that Harriet Mary takes a tone of optimism and industriousness. She does not want to inspire displeasure or disappointment. But even with a clear purpose of seeking approval from her teachers, she manages to incorporate her complaints about going on outing and her critiques of the Euro-Americans she observes.

Harriet Mary's first sign of discomfort comes immediately after she politely inquires after Pratt's whereabouts. She writes: "I am very glad to get here it is a very beautiful place to stay, very pretty out side but in my room where I stay is not clean its [sic] looks as if they were spilling some sugar on the floor and I have got only one sheet in my bed and the blanket smells very badly and I took the sheet to cover me all over." Her comments focus on the landscape but then turn to the contrasting interior space. Her room is some kind of storage or food preparation area where sugar has been spilled. She expresses dismay at the dirty appearance and bad smells of her living quarters and implies that she is too cold at night because she has to choose between sleeping under a foul-smelling blanket or shivering beneath a thin sheet. This passage speaks to the physical discomfort and suffering a servant would experience, not the care a surrogate family member would receive. It also demonstrates an embodied rhetorical mode. While she cannot object verbally to her outing, her body speaks for her with its catalog of feelings: bad smells, shivering, the feeling of sticky sugar on her feet. As Jay Dolmage (2009, 2) has argued, "rhetoric has a body—has bodies," and our goal as scholars is to "create rhetorical exigence for bodies that have been overlooked and Othered." Here, an embodied rhetoric shows Harriet Mary's resistant stance toward her outing experience. Like Ernest White Thunder and Charles Kihega, she uses her body to speak the truths her words alone cannot express due to the constraints of her rhetorical situation.

Lest she appear ungrateful, Harriet Mary turns again to the valleys around her that "looked very beautiful to me." She continues: "I liked to stay here very much. I don't care how the blanket smells. I want to say this that if the things don't shoot me well I have to do it I want to try to be a brave girl and not be afraid to work hard." As her syntax picks up speed and flows together in this final sentence, we can infer her turn to lessons she picked up at school. Hard work is the most important quality she can exhibit. She seems even to have picked up an English idiom, a version of "that which does not kill me makes me stronger:" "if the things don't shoot me well I have to do it." But in her version, we see the added violence of a weapon and a sense of resigned obligation. "Well I have to do it." I imagine this writer turned to letter writing out of despair and homesickness and managed to find some comfort in pleasing her teachers by demonstrating what she had learned from them. Perhaps these lines functioned as a small comfort, a way to make the filthy room and cold nights tolerable.

When Harriet Mary turns to her thoughts about the white children she has met, her critique is even less subtle. She observes: "I go to Sunday School and church but its [*sic*] very different to me in the Sunday School the children come in they begin to run to their seats, just as if they did'nt [*sic*] know anything. I am glad the Indian boys and girls don't rush to their seats they behave better I think." Here we see Harriet Mary taking pride in the actions of her peers at Carlisle and critiquing the unruliness of white children. On the one hand, we can read this moment as the success of Carlisle behavioral training. This young girl has absorbed lessons of Euro-American decorum and politeness. On the other hand, this is a moment when she can wage a critique in the language of her teachers, simultaneously setting herself and her Native peers above white children while exhibiting what she has learned at school. She writes that the white children seem not to know anything. Something is wrong with how they are learning, and the writer can see herself as a child who acts appropriately even in a foreign and difficult situation.

This critique of the white children can also be seen as a critique of the white women who are their mothers, teachers, and caregivers. The outing program was intended to create an environment where Native girls could observe white womanhood in practice. As Zink (2015, 48) shows, this domestic education program was meant to "remake American Indian girls into copies of European American women" who would then return to their reservation communities and model Euro-American womanhood to those who had not been to school. If the white women the girls observed lived in filthy houses with sugar on the floor or allowed their children to be unruly and undisciplined, what kind of copy was being made? When the Nez Perce girl critiques her room and her Sunday School teacher, she is actually critiquing the very Euro-American womanhood she is meant to absorb and emulate.

Pratt articulates his view of the important role Native girls would play in his civilizational program in the March 1881 edition of the

School News.[12] The composition in question works through a quote from Secretary of the Interior Carl Schurz and an editorial response by Samuel Townsend. Schurz writes: "Particularly do I believe in the usefulness of [government] schools for Indian girls. The position of these women is the way to the question. The Indians will never be civilized until they are attached to a permanent home and this will only be accomplished by the elevation of their women" (Townsend 1881b). The inclusion of this quote in spring of 1881 speaks to Pratt's growing concern about bringing enough Indian girls to Carlisle when most of the communities from which he recruited students only wanted to send boys. In the winter of that year, he sent telegraphs and wrote letters to the commissioner of Indian affairs insisting that Indian agents and other recruiters focus on obtaining equal numbers of girls and boys from the reservations they visited. He lamented that only 78 girls were attending Carlisle, with boys numbering 155. In one letter to the Indian commissioner, Pratt wrote:

> The success of this kind of work depends more upon the education of an equal number of girls and boys than I fear the Department realizes. I have letters from some of the boys that were with me so long who have taken wives from the camps without any training or education and it is evident that for that reason they find a great many difficulties to contend with in trying to maintain their acquired status that should not be imposed upon them and may sooner or later destroy them. (Letter from Richard Henry Pratt to Commissioner of Indian Affairs Hiram Price, January 28, 1882)

Pratt voices his concern that any cultural change the boys achieve at school cannot be maintained when they return to their homes if girls have not also embraced those changes. Pratt recognizes and fears what Beth Piatote (2013) and Jane Simonsen (2006) have theorized as the role of the domestic in the assimilationist period. For Pratt and his contemporaries, the primary threat to US nation building was the resilience of tribal nations, and that resilience emerged from the Indian home and family (Piatote 2013, 4).

Following the quote from Schurz, editor Samuel Townsend gives his own commentary, which is heavily influenced by Pratt: "If just the Indian boys were educated and the girls not, it would take a long while to civilize the Indians . . . If a boy goes out in his country and has had some schooling, and he gets a wife that has not been at school she would not keep the house clean because she don't [*sic*] know anything about household duties" (Townsend 1881b). When Harriet Mary went into the country for her outing, then, she was meant to perform gendered labor for a rural family and also to observe and mirror how white women behaved. When she speaks to the improper behavior of white children or the dirtiness of her house, Harriet Mary suggests that her white relations are not the ideal after which she will model her domestic life. She feels more kinship with her native friends at school than she does with these white strangers. Although the writer acquiesces to the standards and expectations of her Carlisle "parents," she uses her body to express resistance to the outing process and her words to critique the Euro-American culture she is supposed to replicate. She demonstrates how young Native women pushed back against the dual colonial forces of gendered and linguistic violence, using the language of her body to critique the outing experience, white women's domesticity, and, by extension, the entire Carlisle project.

While the periodical press obscures the identity of this Nez Perce girl, perhaps to suggest that all Carlisle girls had a similar experience in the outing program, it is worth delving into who Harriet Mary was and how she came to be at the school. In fact, Harriet Mary Elder has much in common with the other students whose resistant rhetoric has taken much more obvious forms.[13] On her student information card, we discover that she arrived from the Ponca Reservation in Indian Territory, not the Nez Perce Reservation in Idaho as we might expect. This small detail reveals that she is part of the band of Chief Joseph's followers taken prisoner after the Nez Perce War of 1877. This group resisted removal from its ancestral lands in the Wallowa Valley in Oregon to the smaller Idaho Nez Perce Reservation. Violent encounters with settlers led Chief Joseph's band to flee and seek asylum in Canada with the Lakota led by Sitting Bull who had been in exile there for four years after defeating Custer at the Battle of the Greasy Grass (Little Big Horn). Seven hundred men, women, and children engaged in a series of armed conflicts as they fled toward Canada, but in October 1877, the US Army cornered the band in northern Montana territory. They surrendered under the condition that they be allowed to return to the reservation in western Idaho; instead, the party was confined as prisoners of war in Fort Leavenworth for eight months and then sent to the Ponca Reservation for seven years.[14]

Harriet Mary Elder arrived in Carlisle on February 20, 1880. At age thirteen, she had been on the run from the US government or confined in military prison or on a foreign reservation for much of her young life. Two years later, at the time of her outing, she certainly had not forgotten her childhood experiences. Like Ernest White Thunder, Luther Standing Bear, and Plenty Horses, she was the child of leaders who refused to acquiesce to settler incursions on their land, instead deploying tactics of war and resorting to migration to resist the overwhelming force of the US government. She found herself at school in a thinly veiled hostage situation and did what she could to stay alive among those who had dispossessed her people. Understanding this part of her story illuminates how much Carlisle students had to obscure in their texts to survive their rhetorical situations. A reader unfamiliar with Harriet Mary's history as a child of Nimiipuu (Nez Perce) resisters would likely assume that she was a successfully assimilated student. Only through her embodied rhetorics do we begin to glimpse the deep ambivalence this fifteen-year-old letter writer must have experienced during her time on Pennsylvania farms.

When Harriet Mary arrived at the school, she was one of two Nimiipuu girls from the Ponca Reservation. The other child was called Sophia Rachel. Unlike Luther Standing Bear, we do not know how these girls acquired their names. It is clear, however, that their names are fully Americanized and do not denote their family members as many of the other students' names do (Ernest White Thunder, for example, had his father's name assigned as his last name by Carlisle staff). It is strange that neither girl has a last name, an anomaly at the school at this time. Perhaps their parents had died, or perhaps Pratt assigned them only first names to erase their previous kinship ties and keep their identities in suspended animation until they married and took on the patrilineal marker of their husbands' surnames. On Harriet Mary's student information card, inscribed slightly above "Harriet Mary" we find the last name Elder, which looks to have been added later. On the same card, we note that Harriet Mary went on an outing with Rebecca O. Elder in Harrisburg, Pennsylvania, from July 13, 1883, to January 26, 1884.[15] Harriet Mary, then, took on the surname of one of her outing supervisors and kept that name until her marriage to James Stuart after leaving school. The ambiguity of Harriet Mary's position is nowhere clearer than in her chosen name. While her writings indicate her capacity to critique the assimilationist project, she also embraces many affective aspects of Carlisle's domestic curriculum. She may have taken on the name of a white patron as a way of indicating her process of acculturation into American society.

As Harriet Mary got older, she continued to engage with and perform assimilation in complicated and ambivalent ways. She left Carlisle in 1886 after going on three extended outing periods, the first of which she talks about in her letter discussed above. She ended up at the Nez Perce Reservation in Idaho, the reservation from which her band was barred because of its refusal to remove there in 1877. Her relatives remained in Oklahoma.[16] After six years at school, she "returned" to a place that had never been her home and a community that was not her own. She reported back to Carlisle regularly over the years as administrators sent out cards to ascertain what their students were doing. In 1911—twenty-five years after leaving Carlisle—she, now Harriet Mary Stuart, reported being a housewife in Kooskia, Idaho, where her husband, James, worked as a civil engineer. Her husband was also a returned student, a graduate of the Chemawa boarding school in Oregon. She filled out cards in 1910 and 1913 with similar information about her life and in 1915 attached an article she wrote for the *Nez Perce Indian* titled "Making Our Homes Attractive."[17]

This article argues that Indian homes should be managed in ways that mirror the domestic norms of the white middle class because a well-managed and manicured home will prove that Indians are equal to Euro-Americans:

> Let us try to show the white people we can have just as good and clean homes as any body, and have our surroundings just as attractive as any. All returned students from Carlisle, Chemawa, and other non-reservation schools should do their best and take the lead among our people to keep the homes clean . . . Some people may point a finger at us and say we are too proud but let us go ahead and use what we have learned in school to the best of our ability. The people will fall in line after awhile if we keep our courage up. (Stuart 1915)

Much of Harriet Mary's writing as an adult, both in her information cards and in her article, registers some discomfort with her Nimiipuu community and her outsider status. Here, for example, she implies that her domestic practices received pejorative comments from her neighbors and that she has to "keep her courage up" to practice her boarding school training.

But she also uses her time at school as a way to bridge traditional practices with a future for Indigenous peoples. In the following passage on Native thrift, Harriet Stuart wages an acute critique of settler-colonial wastefulness and violence while also arguing for a Native take on the assimilationist lesson of "thrift":

> To be saving need not mean stinginess, which the Indian abhors. In his native state he was not wasteful. It was not he, but the white man, who killed off the buffalo. Neither was it he who cut down forests and destroyed the game. To this day he is twice as saving of fuel as the white man, and he does not kill and skin a deer for a hunting trophy merely, leaving the carcass to the coyotes. If this native thrift could be applied to the things of modern life the future of the Indian would be safe. (Stuart 1915)

As in her letter disparaging the Euro-American home and church in relation to Carlisle and its Native students, Harriet Stuart critiques settler lifeways while embracing practices of domestic assimilation. In her refusal to accept either the supremacy of Euro-American culture or a static notion of Nez Perce domesticity, she shares much with other Native American women writing political journalism in the Assimilation Era. As Carol Batker (1996, 191) has argued, these writers "accepted integrationist policy and at the same time developed a rhetoric of Native rights that assumed a separate Native identity." For Batker, these journalistic writings demonstrate "cultural dynamism rather than cultural loss as a paradigm for assimilation" (190). Harriet Stuart's texts demonstrate the complex rhetorical position of a returned student who embraces her boarding school education while also negotiating the history of settler violence that resulted in that education. Following her return to a Nimiipuu community, she argues that her nation should perform Euro-American cultural practices to move toward equality in the eyes of settler society, a form of protection she surely craved after her youth in exile and imprisonment by the US government. Harriet Mary's writing shows that even the most seemingly assimilated students did not lose their capacity to critique settler society or their fundamental commitment to an Indigenous future on the land occupied by the United States.

The periodical press at Carlisle served as much more than a fundraising and disciplinary device. The *School News* is a repository of Indigenous resourcefulness and survivance, but these features of the periodical are necessarily obfuscated by the realities of surveillance that students faced. For this reason, we risk neglecting the deep well of cultural sustenance Native rhetors draw from under conditions of colonization by focusing on alphabetic text. Rather, we must read these texts in their relation to other forms of expression, particularly embodied forms of critique. Because the *School News* featured obedient and exemplary students, it is also a fascinating place to glimpse the complex negotiations of language and identity that seemingly assimilated students are working through. In particular, this periodical asks us to pay attention to the ways students used the language of their bodies to write their resistance and how this tactic fits within the larger context of embodied Indigenous rhetorics at the center of the study. Charles Kihega and Harriet Mary are young people from nations in crisis at a period of heightened settler violence and land theft. When they came to the school, they must have felt some hope after their youths were spent in chaos, hunger, and war. Both students clearly viewed English literacy as a way to impact the futures of their nations. Charles used that literacy to advocate for his people to remain on their land in Kansas, and Harriet Mary used it to imagine a calm and orderly domestic future for herself as a Nimiipuu woman. Both students engaged alphabetic literacy, the English language, and periodical print to materialize a new relationship between settler and Indigenous cultures: coexistence rather than replacement. It is my hope that the archival and embodied reading practices at work in this chapter will allow composition studies to more fully acknowledge the complicity of literacy education in the colonial enterprise while recognizing the rhetorical resilience of Native American peoples.

Afterword
CARLISLE'S RHETORICAL LEGACY

In the spring of 2018, the Trump administration began its family separation policy at the border between the United States and Mexico. The federal government set up separate detention facilities for migrant parents and their children taken into custody after crossing the border without documents. On social media, activists began drawing connections between child detentions at the border and child detentions in off-reservation boarding schools. One example is an Instagram post created by Georgian Bay Métis artist, activist, and scholar Dylan Miner, posted on Instagram on June 18, 2018. Miner reproduced one of the best-known before-and-after photographs taken by John N. Choate. The side-by-side photographs are of Tom Torlino, a Navajo student who arrived at Carlisle in 1882 and left in 1886 after going on two outings in Andalusia and Cumberland County, Pennsylvania.[1] The photographs are dated 1882 and 1885, repectively, and narrativize a complete transformation. In the "after" photo, Tom Torlino wears a suit, has short hair, and appears to have lighter skin, an effect Barbara Landis and Richard Tritt attribute to manipulations of the lighting in Choate's studio.[2] The images suggest that Torlino's cultural transformation shows up in his body, making it a racial transformation as well.

But in Miner's post, the photographs have come to mean something different. Miner has added text above the images: "settler nations were built by separating families," and below, "silence is complicity in their colonial violence." Within this textual frame, the before-and-after photographs call up the experiences of trauma and coercion that Native youth survived at off-reservation boarding schools. Now, the transformation from savage to student reads as an indictment of settler society. This historical injustice accrues new meaning when connected with the family separation policy of 2018. Miner's image shows that the United States has been here before. It demands that the settler viewer interrogate the impulse to say "this is not who we are." History tells us, this is exactly who we are.

The sepia photographs pull the Unites States loose from its temporal grounding. Myths of a post-racial society are thrown into relief when we

DOI: 10.7330/9781646420872.c005

TOM TORLINO—NAVAJO

As He Entered the School in 1882.   As He Appeared Three Years Later.

Figure 5.1. This side-by-side rendering of the two images of Tom Torlino appears in John N. Choate's Souvenir of the Carlisle Indian School *(Carlisle, PA: J. N. Choate, 1902). Courtesy of the Dickinson College Archives and Special Collections.*

see that the impulse to incarcerate children is returning in a new form. The post suggests that settler notions of linear time and social progress fall short. A new wave of white nationalism is taking shape around us. Unlike Pratt, Miner does not let the images speak for themselves. The words *settler, separating,* and *silence* resonate in their consonance, juxtaposing past and present, demanding that a settler audience see itself clearly. Miner leaves no space for fantasies of benevolence that drown out the reality that the United States is built on stolen land. We cannot move forward, he suggests, until the colonial regime ends and right relations are restored between the human and non-human inhabitants of the American continent.

Richard Pratt would not be pleased to see how his rhetorical legacy has reemerged. I imagine that he would want to explain himself, to remind us that he believed completely in the rightness of his project. He planned, after all, that his students would only have to give up their national identities in exchange for full citizenship in the United States. But Pratt is not here to defend himself. All that remains are the images and texts he produced. He could not control what those images would mean in the publics that emerged in the twentieth and twenty-first centuries. In this sense, his rhetorical project failed. He did not imagine what new possibilities would grow from the seeds of intertribal relations that were planted at school. He did not imagine that his students would survive their education and use the new techniques they learned at school to resist the ongoing colonization of their land.

While the before-and-after photos have an afterlife in the digital environment, Fort Marion prisoners' drawings continue to afford Native artists a space to shift relations between Indigenous nations and the United States. In 2015, curators Emily Arthur, Marwin Begaye, and John Hitchcock commissioned work from seventy-two Native and non-Native artists to mirror the seventy-two prisoners who were detained at Fort Marion. The exhibition was called *Re-Riding History: From the Southern Plains to the Matanzas Bay*. All of the pieces shared a common media: artists used paper in the same dimensions of the ledger drawings made by Etahdleuh Doanmoe and his comrades. Much like Miner's reframing of Tom Torlino's photographs, these artworks challenge the past-ness of the history of assimilationist education. *Re-Riding History* appeared around the country, beginning in St. Augustine in 2015 and culminating in Carlisle, Pennsylvania, in 2018, marking the centennial of the closing of the school as well as the route assimilationist policies took in the late nineteenth century. The artists' works demonstrate how prisoners' and students' techniques of cultural persistence far outlasted the assimilationist movement. *Re-Riding History* is a testament to how relational rhetorics travel through time, accruing new meaning and contributing to collective memory and collective action.

Art historian Nancy Marie Mithlo is a descendent of the Apaches who made up Geronimo's band. This group, now known as the Fort Sill Chiricahua Warm Springs Apache tribe, was imprisoned at Fort Marion, then Mount Vernon Barracks, Alabama, and finally Fort Sill, Oklahoma, for a total of twenty-eight years. Pratt recruited many of their children for Carlisle, a number of whom died at the school. Of the *Re-Riding History* exhibition, Mithlo (2018, 34) writes:

> The total process of exhibit planning is a type of ceremony in which many people are led into a shared activity . . . by the curators whose vision inspired the project. Their actions, their thoughts, over an extended period of months, or in this case even years, have the capacity to give honor and respect to these lives that were stolen from us and whose pain continues to influence our lives today.

Mithlo articulates how the exhibition serves as a communal practice of memory and healing. This ceremony is made possible by the rhetorical practices of the Plains Indian prisoners who encoded their stories in pictographic writing on ledger paper. Because Pratt and his contemporaries did not understand how to read these texts, they valued them as relics of a dying race and preserved them in an act of what Philip J. Deloria (1998) calls salvage ethnography. The messages encoded by these prisoners reemerge, just as they imagined they would. The relational media of Plains pictography allows contemporary Native artists and communities to revisit and revitalize the prisoners' stories in new forms. These media accrue meaning today precisely because of their historical significance for Plains peoples in the violent crisis that culminated in the Fort Marion incarcerations. This rhetoric of relations lives on, continuing to serve the descendants of the men and women the US military imagined they assimilated.

Let us come full circle. I close with two pieces from the exhibition that demonstrate how Indigenous media from Fort Marion and Carlisle are circulating, making meaning, and shifting relations today. The first piece is by Hock E Aye Vi, Edgar Heap of Birds (Cheyenne/Arapahoe). Heap of Birds's great-great-grandfather, Chief Many Magpies, was a prisoner at Fort Marion. For *Re-Riding History*, the artist contributes a mono print presenting "Grandfather" in the Cheyenne language three times:

NUMSHIM

NUMSHIM

NUMSHIM

Many Magpies was one of the four principal chiefs of the Cheyenne at the time of his incarceration. He died at Fort Marion and is buried somewhere nearby. Heap of Birds (2014) says the piece "can be seen as a cry or longing for the loss of Grandfather, a lamenting." The print reaches backward in time, grieving for a lost relative who was taken from his family and who died in the custody of the US government. It also creates a genealogy of grandfathers, a chronology of relatives. Heap of Birds (2018) explains, "Also the words speak of my Cheyenne Grandfathers: Guy Heap of Birds, Alfrich Blackwolf Heap of Birds, Chief Many Magpies Heap O Birds." The print is a ceremony of mourning. It is also a celebration of Cheyenne life, art, and persistence. The print depicts a long history of Cheyenne presence, a presence made visible by the bright red print of Many Magpies's descendant. When the prisoners of war told their stories in ledger books, they envisioned a future audience for their texts. Heap of Birds shows that they did not dream in vain. The Cheyenne continue their ancestors' rhetorical and artistic practices. They continue to shift those practices to respond to new exigencies and possibilities for survivance.

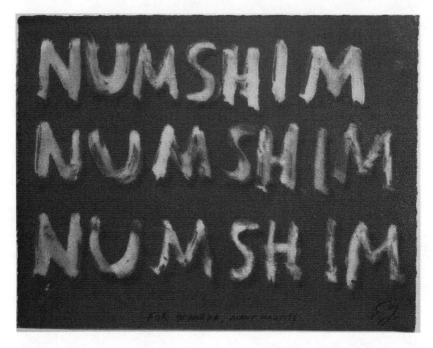

Figure 5.2. Edgar Heap of Birds, For Grandpa, Many Magpies. *Displayed at the Trout Gallery, the art museum of Dickinson College in Carlisle, Pennsylvania, from June 1 to October 27, 2018, as part of the* Re-Riding History *exhibit.*

The stories told in this book also resonate with Muscogee (Creek) artist Bobby C. Martin's piece, *Pursuit of Civilization #5.* Martin (2018) says of the piece:

> Koba was taught to read and write in English, and it is from one of his pages of carefully practiced cursive writing lessons that I selected to use as the foundation for my artwork. The piece, using a photo-etching process, combines an image from my own family's past, a young man who attended Dwight Indian Training School in Vian, Oklahoma in the early 20th century. Many of my relatives attended various Indian schools, so I became very interested in Koba's experiences and his connection to the formation of schools created to give our ancestors a "proper education."

I am fascinated by Martin's re-presentation of Koba's language-learning text. By underlaying this archival document, he connects Fort Marion, Carlisle, and the many other Indian schools that followed these early models, including the school his relatives attended. Martin draws on the evocative nature of an archival, handwritten document and overlays a recognizable "after" photograph of a young man who experienced the assimilationist

Figure 5.3. Bobby C. Martin, Pursuit of Civilization #5. *Displayed at the Trout Gallery, the art museum of Dickinson College in Carlisle, Pennsylvania, from June 1 to October 27, 2018, as part of the* Re-Riding History *exhibit.*

movement. Through these visible layers, Martin elegantly demonstrates how the rhetorical modes of Euro-Americans (English alphabetic writing and photography) changed in the hands of Indigenous rhetors.

Koba's partially obscured document looks much like the slate of Rutherford B. Hayes found in this book's introduction—there is a series of words with corresponding pictures next to them (roof, flat, flower, flour) and a draft of a letter at the bottom of the page. Up the side, we can see what appears to be an English phrase that moves into Kiowa—"gone don gya go"—followed by the image of a head, the word *Kiowa*, and a drawing of a man resting his back on what looks like a copse of trees. We can see how Koba augments his rhetorical resources, building his communicative repertoire and writing the name of his nation in the alphabetic text of his captors. In other words, he is envisioning, drafting, and creating new relations between his Kiowa language and the English words he is learning, between his Plains media and his Euro-American ledger page. Martin's piece is a layering of language, history, and media that demonstrates how Indigenous rhetors incorporated Euro-American modes into their existing means of expression to tell their stories and imagine a future for their nations.

What does it mean for these re-imaginings of Carlisle and Fort Marion to circulate today, augmenting the marks Indigenous rhetors made in carceral institutions a century before? How do contemporary artists realize the hopes of the prisoners and students who encoded their experiences so that future generations could make meaning from their stories? How did that encoding process itself create the possibility that there would be future generations for whom these marks would be legible? These are the questions raised by the remarkable artists responding to the legacy of the rhetors from Fort Marion and Carlisle.

We are living in a moment of Indigenous political resurgence. Water protectors are blocking the construction of oil pipelines in highly visible efforts such as the #NoDAPL movement led by the Standing Rock Sioux, the same nation that coordinated resistance to the Dawes Act in 1887. The Idle No More movement, a coalition of First Nations activists in Canada, was galvanized when Chief Theresa Spence of the Attawapiskat First Nation went on a hunger strike in 2012, a tactic deployed nearly 150 years prior by Lean Bear and Ernest White Thunder during their respective incarcerations. In 2019, scientists planned to build a telescope on the peaks of Mauna Kea, a sacred site for the Kanaka Maoli, or Native Hawaiians, and thousands of protesters assembled to block construction. They quickly established Puuhonua o Puuhuluhulu University, a free, de-colonial model for education and a corrective to the epistemic violence Hawaiians have faced through assimilationist education. Each of these movements realizes the promise of the students I have discussed in this book—a future when Indigenous lifeways will continue. This has been a story about techniques of survivance, processes of resistance, and a vision for Indigenous futurity against one of the most horrific genocidal campaigns of the US settler state. The legacy of Fort Marion and Carlisle rhetors lives on in the ongoing resistance of Indigenous peoples to settler-colonialism.

NOTES

PREFACE

1. From the Report to the House of Representatives from the Indian Committee 46th Congress, 2nd Session, Report no. 752: "It is claimed for this school that it serves a double purpose—first, as an educator of those who are here, and, second, as an educating and controlling influence over the Indians of the West. It is plain that they will feel a lively interest in an institution which shelters and provides for their children. It is also plain that the fact of having here so many children of chiefs and headmen is an effectual guarantee of the good behavior of the tribes represented" (Pratt 1880b, 1).

2. Warrior (2005, 107) distinguishes pan-Indianism, which he argues seeks to homogenize Indian cultures, from intertribalism, which values respect towards both particularity and sameness among different tribes.

INTRODUCTION: TOWARD A RHETORIC OF RELATIONS

1. Information cards for both boys are available online through the Carlisle Indian School Digital Resource Center. They both entered school on October 27, 1879. At that time, R. B. Hayes was fourteen and John Williams was twelve.

2. In 1892, Pratt delivered a speech to the Nineteenth Annual Conference of Charities and Correction in which he articulated his now famous motto: "[A] great general has said that the only good Indian is a dead one, and that high sanction of his destruction has been an enormous factor in promoting Indian massacres. In a sense, I agree with the sentiment, but only in this: that all the Indian there is in the race should be dead. Kill the Indian in him, and save the man." Pratt's speech is included in the Official Report of the Nineteenth Annual Conference of Charities and Correction, 46–59 (Pratt 1973).

3. For more on Carlisle photographs and the assimilationist project, see Wexler (1994).

4. Mary Louise Pratt (1992, 6) defines the contact zone as "the space of colonial encounters, the space in which peoples geographically and historically separated come into contact with each other and establish ongoing relations, usually involving conditions of coercion, radical inequality, and intractable conflict."

5. The shift to New Literacy Studies in the 1980s marked the move from the oppositional "literacy" and "orality" to situated concepts like Scribner and Cole's "literacy practices" (1981) and Shirley Bryce Heath's "literacy events" (1988). Brian Street (1995) demonstrated the ideological implications of how we think about writing through his critique of the Great Divide thesis and reevaluated the myriad ways a society can maintain knowledge over time. Despite correctives offered by New Literacy Studies, however, our field still needs to account for centuries of colonial mythology passing as literacy scholarship. Totalizing theories of literacy and orality remain central to scholarly conversations about the history of rhetoric, and decolonizing scholarship is too often seen as a subfield or a special interest that is only a part of the still Western-centric fields of literacy and rhetorical studies. The history

of rhetoric maps onto the history of colonization since 1492, and the project of fully integrating non-Western communicative practices and perspectives into the broader field remains incomplete.

6.   Philip H. Round's (2010, 4) work, for example, illuminates not only pre-contact forms of graphic communication, from Haudenosaunee wampum belts to Great Plains hide paintings, but also two centuries (1663–1880) during which "Native peoples in North American had begun to devise hundreds of ways to exploit the European technologies of alphabetic literacy and printed books for their own ends."

7.   When Carlisle policies and curriculum overlay body and language, they show how the meaning of disability is contingent on historical conditions. Douglas C. Baynton (1996, 33, original emphasis) argues that "disability has functioned historically to justify inequality for disabled people themselves, but . . . the *concept* of disability has been used to justify discrimination against other groups by attributing disability to them." Categories of disability and ethnicity are inextricable when colonialism is justified through a belief in the cultural/intellectual superiority of the colonizer. John Duffy and Melanie Yergeau (2011) propose that rhetoric functions as a powerfully shaping instrument for creating conceptions of identity and positioning individuals relative to established social and economic hierarchies. A function of the rhetorical scholar is to identify such powerfully shaping instruments and their effects on individuals, including disabled individuals. Duffy and Yergeau show how rhetoric constructs social identifications and power relations. And if, as Dolmage and Chávez would insist, rhetoric has a body, then the possible means of communication are always determined by discourses of physical abnormality. When rhetorics of disability and indigeneity overlap, as they did in assimilationist literacy training, we can see how language education can pathologize vulnerable bodies through their means of communication.

8.   See Bruchac (2018); Cushman (2011); Fitzgerald (2008).

CHAPTER 1: PLAINS PICTOGRAPHY AND EMBODIED RESISTANCE AT FORT MARION

1.   Historian Greg Grandin (2019, 4) argues that prior to the Civil War, the shifting Western frontier "allowed the United States to avoid a true reckoning with its social problems, such as economic inequality, racism, crime and punishment, and violence." Frederick Jackson Turner's frontier thesis (1921) also posited that American democracy functioned primarily due to a shared American identity based in the promise of perpetual further expansion. As expansion reached the boundaries of the continent following the Spanish-American War, imperial desires turned to the Dominican Republic, Haiti, Nicaragua, the Philippines, and Puerto Rico; but a less discussed expansionist potential appears in the allotment of tribal land that breaks up tribal landholdings into private property that could be more easily purchased by settlers.

2.   The name is spelled Minimic in Stowe's piece.

3.   Hayes Peter Mauro (2011, 41) has noted that the casts taken by Mills were originally intended to appear atop mannequins dressed in Native American clothing in a "Hall of Native Peoples" to reinforce the scientific legitimacy of the scenes in the Smithsonian Institution's Natural History Museum. The casts became ethnographic objects that were used to advance new forms of scientific racism emerging in the study of criminology. The Smithsonian's second secretary, Spencer F. Baird, asked Pratt to catalog the specific atrocities committed by each of the sixty-four prisoners whose casts were made, as well as their height, weight, age, tribe, tribal rank, name, and

so-called racial makeup (Mauro 2011, 49). Clark Mills, the artist who created the casts, drew on the earlier pseudo-science of phrenology to argue against Pratt's belief in the prisoners' educability: "When I began taking the casts of the Indians I found the size of the brain fully up to the average of the white race—I thought all that was necessary for them was education, but as I advanced I found that one set of [phrenological] organs were [*sic*] more fully developed than the others . . . It seems that those largely developed organs having been cultivated over so many generations have become permanent, they are transmitted to posterity" (quoted in Mauro 2011, 51).

4. Stereographs were an early form of three-dimensional photograph popular in the late nineteenth century. According to the American Antiquarian Society, "Placed on cardboard were two almost identical photographs, side by side, to be viewed with a stereoscope. When viewed through a stereoscope, the photograph appeared three-dimensional, an awe-inspiring illusion for anyone during that time." https://www.americanantiquarian.org/stereographs.htm.

5. The Miriam and Ira D. Wallach Division of Art, Prints, and Photographs: Photography Collection, New York Public Library Digital Collections, New York City. Accessed February 18, 2020. http://digitalcollections.nypl.org/items/510d47e0-5380-a3d9-e040-e00a18064a99.

6. Berlo cites unpublished manuscript #0625BB, the Kiowa collection: Selections from the Papers of High [*sic*] Lenox Scott. Manuscript Division, Library of Congress, Washington, DC.

CHAPTER 2: PLAINS SIGN TALK

1. For more on the history of bilingual missionary literacy efforts with Native American tribes, see Bross 2004; Monaghan 2005; Peyer 1997; Wyss 2000, 2012.

2. Pratt's view of indigeneity can be traced back to the first Indian Policy in the United States. George Washington's secretary of war, Henry Knox, believed a civilization program would eventually subsume all tribal identities beneath the purview of American citizenship. Drafted in 1789, Knox's program planned a fifty-year window for Indians east of the Mississippi to integrate into Anglo-American society. By extinguishing titles, denationalizing tribes, and leaving only "individual Indian landholders scattered as farmer-citizens among the whites," Knox believed the question of relations between whites and Indians would be resolved (McLoughlin 1981, 4). This policy reflected the cultural rather than racial divide between Euro-Americans and Indians. Indians were seen as uncivilized simply because they had not been adequately exposed to Euro-American cultural practices. For more on Knox's civilizational program, see McLoughlin (1981).

3. Dolmage (2014, 3) characterizes rhetoric as "the strategic study of the circulation of power through communication." He believes "we should recognize rhetoric as the circulation of discourse through the body" (5). Following Aristotle's famous definition of rhetoric as "the faculty of discovering in any particular case all of the available means of persuasion," Dolmage argues that "the body has never been fully or fairly understood for its role in shaping and multiplying these available means" (3).

CHAPTER 3: LAKOTA STUDENTS' EMBODIED RHETORICS OF REFUSAL

1. While Pratt calls this boy Ernest White Thunder (the first name given to him at Carlisle and the last name—his father's—meant to enforce patrilineal kinship

in the Euro-American tradition), Luther Standing Bear (2006b, 159) recalls him with his honorific Lakota name Wica-karpa, or Knocked-It-Off. For the purposes of referring to him consistently as he appears in the archival materials and existing literature, I use Ernest White Thunder but remain aware that he may not have identified with this name.

2. Held at the Cumberland County Historical Society, this photograph is described as "Portrait of Agnes (White Cow) (Sioux Nation) and Ernest (Knocks Off) (Sioux Nation) posed on the steps of the bandstand on the school grounds. They are the son and sister-in-law of Chief White Thunder. Photo by John N. Choate for his Stereograph series, c. 1879." This description was likely attached by Pratt or Choate, but I have been unable to verify that Agnes White Cow is in fact Ernest's father's sister-in-law in other documents.

3. Trowbridge died on April 20, 1881, in the middle of the controversy surrounding the children's deaths. President Garfield, who had just taken office on March 4, 1881, appointed Hiram Price to the position. Shortly thereafter, on July 2, 1881, Garfield was shot and remained bedridden until his death on September 19, 1881. All in all, 1881 was a very turbulent year in the US government, which forms the backdrop of the negotiations and petitions between the Lakota at Rosebud and the Bureau of Indian Affairs at this time.

4. Frank Cushing's parents enlisted the help of the government teacher at Zuni Pueblo to write to Pratt on their behalf. The agent, S. A. Bentley, received the response from Pratt who wrote directly to the Indian agent B. M Thomas and the commissioner of Indian affairs that the boy's remains would not be sent home at that time.

5. Oliver and Pollock re-enrolled on November 30, 1882, with Gertrude. Max re-enrolled a year later, on November 13, 1883. Gertrude died on an outing in Byberry, New York, on August 31, 1883. Oliver was discharged and sent home due to ill health on April 10, 1883. Max was discharged due to ill health on July 14, 1885. Both Oliver and Max died shortly after returning to Rosebud. Pollock stayed at Carlisle for his entire term and was discharged on June 27, 1887. Information on the enrollment, death, and/or discharge of each child is available in student information cards digitized at the Carlisle Indian School Digital Resource Center: http://carlisleindian.dickinson.edu/.

6. Although the Dawes Act passed in Congress in 1887, tribal nations are not automatically subject to the laws passed by Congress and there had to be further negotiations with tribes as to how they would allot their land based on stipulations in the earlier 1868 treaty. The Pratt commission and later the Crook commission had to get three-quarters of men residing on the Great Sioux reservation to sign the Allotment Act for it to go into effect in Sioux territory, which they achieved through the 1889 Sioux Agreement.

7. The Ghost Dance movement began after Paiute Holy Man Wovoka had a vision in January 1889. He prophesied that "dead relatives and the buffalo nations would once again walk the earth" and foretold the end of settler presence on the continent and the return of the Oceti Sakowin way of life (quoted in Estes 2019, 123). When the federal government grew concerned about the popularity of the Ghost Dance, it planned to arrest a number of chiefs to quell the movement. James McLaughlin, agent at the Standing Rock Agency, took matters into his own hands and sent a group of Indian police to arrest Sitting Bull, who was shot and killed in the process. As members of Sitting Bull's Hunkpapa band fled, they joined Chief Spotted Elk at the Cheyenne River Reservation and began the journey to Pine Ridge to seek shelter with Red Cloud. During the journey, on December 29, 1890, the coalition encountered a detachment of the Seventh Cavalry, which attempted

to detain and disarm them. They eventually opened fire at close range with Hotch-kiss guns, killing as many as 300 Lakota men, women, and children in what is now called the Wounded Knee Massacre.

8. This quote is reported by former Pine Ridge agent Valentine T. McGillycuddy, who served as foreman of the grand jury that indicted Plenty Horses (Utley 1974). Plenty Horses did not testify at his own trial because the judge insisted that he testify in English and his defense attorneys advised him not to comply. In the literature, Plenty Horses's quote about Carlisle is often attributed to the murder trial, but that is not accurate.

CHAPTER 4: WRITING THEIR BODIES IN THE PERIODICAL PRESS

1. Kaestle (1991, xi) defines the common school as "an elementary school meant to serve all the children in an area. An expensive independent school, obviously, would not be a 'common school,' but neither would a charity school open only to the poor."

2. The American Antiquarian Society holds a large collection of amateur newspapers from around the country including issues of the *School News* and *Everybody's Hand-Book*. Historical context and statistical overview for this collection is provided by Dennis R. Laurie, reference specialist of newspapers and periodicals, and can be found at http://www.americanantiquarian.org/amateurnews.htm.

3. To make sense of students using the *School News* as a means of tribal continuance, we need a broader understanding of how Indigenous peoples embraced and revised periodical print culture between the Removal Period and the Allotment Period within which this study falls. The *Cherokee Phoenix*, a bilingual periodical printed in the Cherokee syllabary and English, is the most prominent example of how Native nations took up the periodical as a site of rhetorical sovereignty. Students at Carlisle were certainly more restricted in how they could use the periodical to expand and communicate their sovereignty, but in some ways, the *Schools News* is taking part in a long Indigenous culture of print. I read Carlisle periodicals within a genealogy of the periodical in Indian Country and look beyond the narrative of assimilation that often characterizes a surface reading of Carlisle texts. These newspapers are but a single link in a long chain of intercultural print practices.

4. According to his information card, Charles Kihega came to Carlisle from the Great Nehama Agency on February 25, 1880, and was discharged on June 10, 1884. The card shows that he was away from school on a home visit from July 19, 1882, until September 23, 1882. In the summer of 1883, he went on outing to a farm near Carlisle in Cumberland County, Pennsylvania. Carlisle student information cards are digitized and available from the Carlisle Indian School Digital Resource Center at http://carlisleindian.dickinson.edu/.

5. Editorial published in the *School News*, Carlisle Indian School, 1 (5) (October 1880), 2. The author is unknown, but may be Samuel Townsend, who was the editor at this time.

6. An 1861 treaty among the US government, the Iowa, and the Sac and Fox Nation required the Iowa to cede land to the Sac and Foxes. In return, the US government would open a school for the Indians (Article 5). http://sacandfoxnation-nsn.gov/sites/sfnation/uploads/documents/SF_CODES_Law/Sauk_treaties/March_6_1863.PDF.

7. All exact quotations from Charles are from this letter (Kihega 1882b), until indicated otherwise later in this section when they switch to the essay from the September issue of the *School News*.

8. Subsequent quotations from Charles are taken from this essay (Kihega 1882a), printed in the *School News* after Charles returned to Carlisle.

9. Brosius writes in the letter that Chief Kihega will come to Carlisle on his way back to Nebraska from Washington, DC, if Charles cannot join him. He did indeed visit Carlisle in April 1882.

10. For more on Iowa territorial losses over the course of the nineteenth century, see Blaine 1995.

11. All direct quotes from Harriet Mary come from this letter (Elder 1882) until otherwise indicated.

12. To clarify, the author is probably Samuel Townsend but Pratt oversaw the editorial and it represents his views.

13. Only two Nez Perce girls could have been in school for two-and-a-half years at the time of the letter's writing (summer 1882). Sophia Rachel arrived with Harriet Mary Elder on February 20, 1880, but was discharged due to ill health on July 1, 1882. Elder went on three outings according to her information card and was on outing in Bellafonte, Pennsylvania, in September 1882; hence my conclusion that this is the girl referred to in the publication.

14. For more on the Nez Perce War, see Brown 1982.

15. Harriet Mary Elder student information card, 1880. Manuscript. Archives and Special Collections, Dickinson College, Carlisle, PA.

16. As late as 1915, Harriet Mary's family was still living in Oklahoma, as indicated by a column she wrote in the *Nez Perce Indian*: "I am planning a trip to visit some of my relatives in Oklahoma and I imagine I will not see so many pretty flowers as we can raise right here in Idaho." Stuart (1915).

17. The Carlisle Indian School Digital Resource Center includes all documents relating to a specific student in a single file, and this allows a fuller picture of Harriet Mary Elder's life before, during, and after her time at Carlisle. Her folder currently includes her student information card, her article in the *Nez Perce Indian*, a completed "Record of Graduates and Returned Students" completed on a typewriter in 1911, a handwritten card reporting on her life in 1913, and a Carlisle record of her status in 1910 and 1913 on a card.

AFTERWORD: CARLISLE'S RHETORICAL LEGACY

1. Tom Torlino student information card, 1882. Manuscript. Archives and Special Collections, Dickinson College, Carlisle, PA.

2. Landis and Tritt (archivist and photograph curator at the Cumberland County Historical Society) are cited as making this point in a Radiolab podcast on the Carlisle school. For more information, see Farrell (2015).

REFERENCES

"An Act to Provide for the Allotment of Lands in Severalty to Indians on the Various Reservations, and to Extend the Protection of the Laws of the United States and the Territories over the Indians, and for Other Purposes." n.d. https://avalon.law.yale.edu /19th_century/dawes.asp.

Adams, David Wallace. 1995. *Education for Extinction: American Indians and the Boarding School Experience 1875–1928.* Lawrence: University Press of Kansas.

Anderson, Benedict. 1991. *Imagined Communities: Reflections on the Origin and Spread of Nationalism.* New York: Verso.

Archuleta, Margaret, Brenda J. Child, and K. Tsianina Lomawaima, eds. 2000. *Away from Home: American Indian Boarding School Experiences, 1879–2000.* Phoenix: Heard Museum.

Baca, Damián. 2010. "Te-Ixtli: The 'Other Face' of the Americas." In *Rhetorics of the Americas, 3114 BCE to 2012 CE,* edited by Damián Baca and Victor Villanueva, 1–14. New York: Palgrave Macmillan.

Batker, Carol. 1996. "Overcoming All Obstacles: The Assimilation Debate in Native American Women's Journalism of the Dawes Era." In *Early Native American Writing: New Critical Essays,* edited by Helen Jaskoski, 190–203. Cambridge: Cambridge University Press.

Baynton, Douglas C. 1996. *Forbidden Signs: American Culture and the Campaign against Sign Language.* Chicago: University of Chicago Press.

Baynton, Douglas C. 2006. "'The Undesirability of Admitting Deaf Mutes': US Immigration Policy and Deaf Immigrants, 1882–1924." *Sign Language Studies* 6 (4): 391–415.

Bellin, Joshua David, and Laura Mielke, eds. 2011. *Native Acts: Indian Performance, 1603–1832.* Lincoln: University of Nebraska Press.

Berlo, Janet Catherine. 2007a. "A Kiowa's Odyssey: Etahdleuh Doanmoe, Transcultural Perspectives, and the Art of Fort Marion." In *A Kiowa's Odyssey,* edited by Phillip Earenfight, 171–197. Seattle: University of Washington Press.

Berlo, Janet Catherine. 2007b. "A Kiowa's Odyssey: Page-by-Page." In *A Kiowa's Odyssey,* edited by Phillip Earenfight, 144–170. Seattle: University of Washington Press.

Bernardin, Susan. 1997. "The Lessons of a Sentimental Education: Zitkála-Šá's Autobiographical Narratives." *Western American Literature* 32 (3): 212–238.

Blaine, Martha Royce. 1995. *The Ioway Indians.* Norman: University of Oklahoma Press.

Branson, Jan, and Don Miller. 2002. *Damned for Their Difference: The Cultural Construction of Deaf People as Disabled.* Washington, DC: Gallaudet University Press.

Bratta, Phil, and Malea Powell. 2016. "Introduction to the Special Issue: Entering the Cultural Rhetorics Conversations." *Enculturation: A Journal of Rhetoric, Writing, and Culture.* http://enculturation.net/entering-the-cultural-rhetorics-conversations.

Brodhead, Richard. 1993. *Cultures of Letters: Scenes of Reading and Writing in Nineteenth-Century America.* Chicago: University of Chicago Press.

Brooks, Lisa. 2008. *The Common Pot: The Recovery of Native Space in the Northeast.* Minneapolis: University of Minnesota Press.

Bross, Kristina. 2004. *Dry Bones and Indian Sermons: Praying Indians in Colonial America.* Ithaca: Cornell University Press.

Brown, Mark Herbert. 1982. *The Flight of the Nez Perce.* Lincoln: University of Nebraska Press.

Bruchac, Margaret. 2018. "Broken Chains of Custody: Possessing, Dispossessing, and Repossessing Lost Wampum." *Proceedings of the American Philosophical Society* 62 (1):

DOI: 10.7330/9781646420872.c006

56–105. https://www.amphilsoc.org/sites/default/files/2018-08/attachments/Bru chac.pdf.

Byrne, Janet. 1869. *Picture Teaching*. New York: Cassell, Petter, and Galpin.

Chávez, Karma R. 2018. "The Body: An Abstract and Actual Rhetorical Concept." *Rhetoric Society Quarterly* 48 (3): 242–250.

Cherokee Nation v. Georgia. 30 US 1 (1831), 2. Supreme Court Collection, Legal Information Inst., Cornell University Law School, Ithaca, NY. https://www.law.cornell.edu /supremecourt/text/30/1.

Child, Brenda J. 1998. *Boarding School Seasons: American Indian Families 1900–1940*. Lincoln: University of Nebraska Press.

Cohen, Matt. 2010. *The Networked Wilderness: Communicating in Early New England*. Minneapolis: University of Minnesota Press.

Crain, Patricia. 2000. *The Story of A: The Alphabetization of America from the New England Primer to the Scarlet Letter*. Stanford, CA: Stanford University Press.

Cram, E. 2016. "Archival Ambience and Sensory Memory: Generating Queer Intimacies in the Settler Colonial Archive." *Communication and Critical/Cultural Studies* 13 (2): 109–129.

Cushman, Ellen. 2011. *The Cherokee Syllabary: Writing the People's Perseverance*. Norman: University of Oklahoma Press.

Cvetkovich, Ann. 2003. *An Archive of Feelings: Trauma, Sexuality, and Lesbian Public Cultures*. Durham, NC: Duke University Press.

Deloria, Philip J. 1998. *Playing Indian*. New Haven, CT: Yale University Press.

Deloria, Philip J. 2011. "Afterword." In *Native Acts: Indian Performance, 1603–1832*, edited by Joshua David Bellin and Laura Mielke, 309–316. Lincoln: University of Nebraska Press.

Dolmage, Jay. 2009. "Metis, Mêtis, Mestiza, Medusa: Rhetorical Bodies across Rhetorical Traditions." *Rhetoric Review* 28 (1): 1–28.

Dolmage, Jay. 2014. *Disability Rhetoric*. Syracuse: Syracuse University Press.

Duffy, John. 2007. *Writing from These Roots: Literacy in a Hmong-American Community*. Honolulu: University of Hawaii Press.

Duffy, John, and Melanie Yergeau. 2011. "Guest Editors' Introduction." *Disability Studies Quarterly* 31 (3). https://dsq-sds.org/article/view/1682/1607.

Earenfight, Phillip. 2007a. "From the Plains to the Coast." In *A Kiowa's Odyssey*, edited by Phillip Earenfight, 12–29. Seattle: University of Washington Press.

Earenfight, Phillip, ed. 2007b. *A Kiowa's Odyssey*. Seattle: University of Washington Press.

Edwards, R.A.R. 2012. *Words Made Flesh: Nineteenth-Century Deaf Education and the Growth of Deaf Culture*. New York: New York University Press.

Elder, Harriet Mary. 1882. Letter published in *School News* 3 (5). Carlisle Indian School, Carlisle, PA. October, 2.

Ellman, Maud. 1993. *The Hunger Artists: Starving, Writing, and Imprisonment*. Cambridge, MA: Harvard University Press.

Emery, Jacqueline, ed. 2017. *Recovering Native American Writings in the Boarding School Press*. Lincoln: University of Nebraska Press.

Enoch, Jessica. 2002. "Resisting the Script of Indian Education: Zitkála-Šá and the Carlisle Indian School." *College English* 65 (2): 117–141.

Enoch, Jessica. 2008. *Refiguring Rhetorical Education: Women Teaching African American, Native American, and Chicano/a Students, 1865–1911*. Carbondale: Southern Illinois University Press.

Estes, Nick. 2019. *Our History Is the Future*. New York: Verso.

Farrell, Brenna. 2015. "Photos: Before and after Carlisle." January 29. https://www .wnycstudios.org/story/photos-before-and-after-carlisle.

Fear-Segal, Jacqueline. 2007. *White Man's Club: Schools, Race, and the Struggle of Indian Acculturation*. Lincoln: University of Nebraska Press.

Fear-Segal, Jacqueline, and Susan D. Rose, eds. 2016. *Carlisle Indian Industrial School: Indigenous Histories, Memories, and Reclamations.* Lincoln: University of Nebraska Press.

Fitzgerald, Stephanie. 2008. "The Cultural Work of a Mohegan Painted Basket." In *Early Native Literacies in New England,* edited by Kristina Bross and Hilary Wyss, 52–56. Amherst: University of Massachusetts Press.

Foucault, Michel. 1979. *Discipline and Punish.* New York: Vintage Books.

Glancy, Diane. 2014. *Fort Marion Prisoners and the Trauma of Native American Education.* Lincoln: University of Nebraska Press.

Gram, John R. 2015. *Education at the Edge of Empire: Negotiating Pueblo Identity in New Mexico's Indian Boarding Schools.* Seattle: University of Washington Press.

Grandin, Greg. 2019. *The End of the Myth: From the Frontier to the Border Wall in the Mind of America.* New York: Metropolitan Books.

Greenblatt, Stephen. 2003. *Marvelous Possessions: The Wonder of the New World.* Oxford: Clarendon.

Haas, Angela. 2015. "Toward a Decolonial Digital and Visual American Indian Rhetorics Pedagogy." In *Survivance, Sovereignty, and Story: Teaching American Indian Rhetorics,* edited by Lisa King, Rose Gubele, and Joyce Rain Anderson, 188–208. Logan: Utah State University Press.

Hasian, Marouf, Jr. 2014. "Biopolitics and Thanatopolitics at Guantánamo, and the Weapons of the Weak in the Lawfare over Force-Feeding." *Law and Literature* 26 (3): 343–364.

Heap of Birds, Edgar. 2018. "Artist Statements and Bios." In *Re-Riding History: From the Southern Plains to the Matanzas Bay,* edited by Phillip Earenfight. Carlisle, PA: Trout Gallery at the Art Museum of Dickinson College. https://www.reridinghistory.org/artist-statements-and-bios.

Heath, Shirley Brice. 1988. "Protean Shapes in Literacy Events." In *Perspectives on Literacy,* edited by Eugene R. Kingten, Barry M. Kroll, and Mike Rose, 91–118. Carbondale: Southern Illinois University Press.

Hertzberg, Hazel W. 1971. *The Search for an American Indian Identity: Modern Pan-Indian Movements.* Syracuse: Syracuse University Press.

Hoxie, Frederick E. 1984. *A Final Promise: The Campaign to Assimilate the Indians, 1880–1920.* Lincoln: University of Nebraska Press.

Iyengar, Malathi Michelle. 2014. "Not Mere Abstractions: Language Policies and Language Ideologies in US Settler Colonialism." *Decolonization: Indigeneity, Education, and Society* 3 (2): 33–59.

Kaestle, Carl F. 1991. *Literacy in the United States: Readers and Reading since 1880.* New Haven, CT: Yale University Press.

Katanski, Amelia. 2005. *Learning to Write "Indian": The Boarding-School Experience and American Indian Literature.* Norman: University of Oklahoma Press.

Keep, John Robinson. 1875. *First Lessons for the Deaf and Dumb.* Hartford, CT: Case, Lockwood, and Brainard.

Kelsey, Penelope. 2013. "Disability and Native North American Boarding School Narratives: Madonna Swan and Sioux Sanitorium." *Journal of Literary and Cultural Disability Studies* 7 (2): 195–212.

Kihega, Charles. 1882a. Essay published in *School News.* Carlisle Indian School, Carlisle, PA. September.

Kihega, Charles. 1882b. Letter published in *School News* 2 (9). Carlisle Indian School, Carlisle, PA. February, 2.

King, Lisa. 2015. "Sovereignty, Rhetorical Sovereignty, and Representation: Keywords for Teaching Indigenous Texts." In *Survivance, Sovereignty, and Story: Teaching American Indian Rhetorics,* edited by Lisa King, Rose Gubele, and Joyce Rain Anderson, 18–34. Logan: Utah State University Press.

Klotz, Sarah. 2014. "The Red Man Has Left No Mark Here: Graves and Land Claim in the Cooperian Tradition." *ESQ: A Journal of the American Renaissance* 60 (3): 328–364.

Kracht, Benjamin R. 2017. *Kiowa Belief and Ritual.* Lincoln: University of Nebraska Press.

Landis, Barbara. 2016. "Naming the Unknowns in the Cemetery." In *Carlisle Indian Industrial School: Indigenous Histories, Memories, and Reclamations,* edited by Jacqueline Fear-Segal and Susan D. Rose, 185–197. Lincoln: University of Nebraska Press.

Landrum, Cynthia. 2019. *The Dakota Sioux Experience at Flandreau and Pipestone Indian Schools.* Lincoln: University of Nebraska Press.

Leap, William. 1993. *American Indian English.* Salt Lake City: University of Utah Press.

Legg, Emily. 2014. "Daughters of the Seminaries: Re-Landscaping History through the Composition Courses at the Cherokee National Female Seminary." *College Composition and Communication* 66 (1): 67–90.

Letter from Augustus Brosius to Richard Henry Pratt. 1882. Manuscript. February 24. Archives and Special Collections, Dickinson College, Carlisle, PA.

Letter from Charles Kihega to the Carlisle Indian School. 1882. Reprinted in *School News* 3 (4): 2. Carlisle Indian School, Carlisle, PA.

Letter from Chief White Thunder to Ernest White Thunder. 1880. Reprinted in *Eadle Keatah Toh.* Carlisle Indian School, Carlisle, PA. April, 1–3.

Letter from Richard Henry Pratt to the Commissioner of Indian Affairs. 1881a. Manuscript. January 26. Archives and Special Collections, Dickinson College, Carlisle, PA.

Letter from Richard Henry Pratt to the Commissioner of Indian Affairs. 1881b. Manuscript. August 11. Archives and Special Collections, Dickinson College, Carlisle, PA.

Letter from Richard Henry Pratt to the Commissioner of Indian Affairs and B. M. Thomas. 1881c. Manuscript. September 30. Archives and Special Collections, Dickinson College, Carlisle, PA.

Letter from Richard Henry Pratt to Commissioner of Indian Affairs Hiram Price. 1882. Manuscript. January 28. Archives and Special Collections, Dickinson College, Carlisle, PA.

Letter from Spotted Tail, Two Strike, White Thunder, and Swift Bear to Agent Cook, with copies sent to the Commissioner of Indian Affairs, the Secretary of the Interior, Richard Pratt, and the President of the United States. 1881. Manuscript. May 23. Archives and Special Collections, Dickinson College, Carlisle, PA.

Letter from White Thunder and Swift Bear to Agent Cook, forwarded to the Commissioner of Indian Affairs. 1880. Manuscript. December 27. Archives and Special Collections, Dickinson College, Carlisle, PA.

Lomawaima, K. Tsianina. 1994. *They Called It Prairie Light: The Story of the Chilocco Indian School.* Lincoln: University of Nebraska Press.

Lomawaima, K. Tsianina, and Teresa L. McCarty. 2006. *To Remain an Indian: Lessons in Democracy from a Century of Native American Education.* New York: Teachers College Press.

Lookingbill, Brad D. 2007. "Because I Want to Be a Man: A Portrait of Etahdleuh Doanmoe." In *A Kiowa's Odyssey,* edited by Phillip Earenfight, 30–56. Seattle: University of Washington Press.

Ludlow, Helen Wilhelmina. "Indian Education at Hampton and Carlisle." 1881. *Harper's New Monthly Magazine* (April): 659–675.

Lurie, Stephen. 2019. "How It Feels to Go on Hunger Strike." *Eater.* https://www.eater.com /2019/3/26/18205475/hunger-strike-oral-history-typhoon-haiyan-climate-change -arab-spring-egypt-spelman-college-daca.

Lyons, Scott Richard. 2000. "Rhetorical Sovereignty: What Do American Indians Want from Writing?" *College Composition and Communication* 51 (3): 447–468.

Lyons, Scott Richard. 2010. *X-Marks: Native Signatures of Assent.* Minneapolis: University of Minnesota Press.

Mann, Henrietta. 1997. *Cheyenne-Arapaho Education, 1871–1982.* Boulder: University Press of Colorado.

Martin, Bobby C. 2018. "Artist Statements and Bios." In *Re-Riding History: From the Southern Plains to the Matanzas Bay,* edited by Phillip Earenfight. Carlisle, PA: Trout Gallery at the

Art Museum of Dickinson College. https://www.reridinghistory.org/artist-statements -and-bios.

Mauro, Hayes Peter. 2011. *The Art of Americanization at the Carlisle Indian School.* Albuquerque: University of New Mexico Press.

McLoughlin, William G. 1981. "Experiment in Cherokee Citizenship, 1817–1829." *American Quarterly* 33 (1): 3–25.

Miner, Dylan. 2018. Wiisaakodewinini. Instagram, June 8. https://www.instagram.com/p/ BkK3cQWAIEU/.

Mithlo, Nancy Marie. 2018. "'The Great Hurt': Pathways to Survival." In *Re-Riding History: From the Southern Plains to the Matanzas Bay,* edited by Phillip Earenfight, 30–37. Carlisle, PA: Trout Gallery at the Art Museum of Dickinson College.

Molin, Paulette Fairbanks. 1998. "'Training the Hand, the Head, and the Heart': Indian Education at Hampton Institute." *Minnesota History* 51: 82–98.

Momaday, N. Scott, and Al Momaday. 1998. *The Way to Rainy Mountain.* Albuquerque: University of New Mexico Press.

Monaghan, E. Jennifer. 2005. *Learning to Read and Write in Colonial America.* Amherst: University of Massachusetts Press.

Montange, Leah. 2017. "Hunger Strikes, Detainee Protest, and the Relationality of Political Subjectivization." *Citizenship Studies* 21 (5): 509–526.

Mt. Pleasant, Alyssa, Caroline Wigginton, and Kelly Wisecup. 2018. "Materials and Methods in Native American and Indigenous Studies: Completing the Turn." *Early American Literature* 53 (2): 407–444.

O'Brien, Jean. 2010. *Firsting and Lasting: Writing Indians Out of Existence in New England.* Minneapolis: University of Minnesota Press.

Peyer, Bernd. 1997. *The Tutor'd Mind: Indian Missionary-Writers in Antebellum America.* Amherst: University of Massachusetts Press.

Piatote, Beth. 2013. *Domestic Subjects: Gender, Citizenship, and Law in Native American Literature.* New Haven, CT: Yale University Press.

Posthumus, David C. 2018. *All My Relatives: Exploring Lakota Ontology, Belief, and Ritual.* Lincoln: University of Nebraska Press.

Powell, Malea. 2002. "Rhetorics of Survivance: How American Indians Use Writing." *College Composition and Communication* 53 (3): 396–434.

Powell, Malea. 2008. "Dreaming Charles Eastman: Cultural Memory, Autobiography, and Geography in Indigenous Rhetorical Histories." In *Beyond the Archives: Research as a Lived Process,* edited by Gesa Kirsch and Liz Rohan, 115–127. Carbondale: Southern Illinois University Press.

Pratt, Mary Louise. 1992. *Imperial Eyes: Travel Writing and Transculturation.* New York: Routledge.

Pratt, Richard Henry. 1880a. "Beginners, Methods, and Progress." *Eadle Keatah Toh* 1 (5). Carlisle Indian School, Carlisle, PA. August, 2.

Pratt, Richard Henry. 1880b. *Eadle Keatah Toh* 1 (1). Carlisle Indian School, Carlisle, PA. January, 4.

Pratt, Richard Henry. 1881. Editorial published in *School News* 1 (10). Carlisle Indian School, Carlisle, PA. March, 2.

Pratt, Richard Henry. 1964. *Battlefield and Classroom: Four Decades with the American Indian, 1867–1904.* New Haven, CT: Yale University Press.

Pratt, Richard Henry. 1973. "The Advantages of Mingling Indians with Whites." In *Americanizing the American Indians,* edited by Francis Paul Prucha, 260–271. Cambridge, MA: Harvard University Press.

Price, Kenneth M., and Susan Belasco Smith, eds. 1995. *Periodical Literature in Nineteenth-Century America.* Charlottesville: University of Virginia Press.

Purdue, Theda, and Michael D. Green. 2005. *The Cherokee Removal: A Brief History with Documents.* Boston: Bedford/St. Martin's.

Rasmussen, Birgit Brander. 2014. "Toward a New Literary History of the West: Etahdleuh Doanmoe's Captivity Narrative." In *Contested Spaces of Early America*, edited by Julianna Barr and Edward Countryman, 257–275. Philadelphia: University of Pennsylvania Press.

Report from Richard Henry Pratt to Commissioner of Indian Affairs Hiram Price. 1882a. Manuscript, January 25. Archives and Special Collections, Dickinson College, Carlisle, PA.

Report from Richard Henry Pratt to Commissioner of Indian Affairs Hiram Price. 1882b. Manuscript, September 30. Archives and Special Collections, Dickinson College, Carlisle, PA.

Rifkin, Mark. 2006. "Romancing Kinship: A Queer Reading of Indian Education and Zitkála-Šá's American Indian Stories." *GLQ: A Journal of Lesbian and Gay Studies* 12 (1): 27–59.

Riley Mukavetz, Andrea, and Malea Powell. 2015. "Making Native Space for Graduate Students: A Story of Indigenous Rhetorical Practice." In *Survivance, Sovereignty, and Story: Teaching American Indian Rhetorics*, edited by Lisa King, Rose Gubele, and Joyce Rain Anderson, 138–159. Logan: Utah State University Press.

Risling Baldy, Cutcha. 2018. *We Are Dancing for You: Native Feminisms and the Revitalization of Women's Coming-of-Age Ceremonies*. Seattle: University of Washington Press.

Round, Philip H. 2010. *Removable Type: Histories of the Book in Indian Country, 1663–1880*. Chapel Hill: University of North Carolina Press.

Royster, Jacqueline Jones, and Gesa E. Kirsch. 2012. *Feminist Rhetorical Practice: New Horizons for Rhetoric, Composition, and Literacy Studies*. Carbondale: Southern Illinois University Press.

Scanlan, Stephen J., Laurie Cooper Stoll, and Kimberly Lumm. 2015. "Starving for Change: The Hunger Strike and Nonviolent Action, 1906–2004." In *Research in Social Movements, Conflicts, and Change*, edited by Patrick G. Coy, 275–323. Bingley, UK: Emerald Publishing Group.

Schultz, Lucille M. 1999. *The Young Composers: Composition's Beginnings in Nineteenth-Century Schools*. Carbondale: Southern Illinois University Press.

Scribner, Sylvia, and Michael Cole. 1981. *The Psychology of Literacy*. Cambridge, MA: Harvard University Press.

Senier, Siobhan. 2001. *Voices of American Indian Assimilation and Resistance*. Norman: University of Oklahoma Press.

Senier, Siobhan. 2012. "Rehabilitation Reservations: Native Narrations of Disability and Community." *Disability Studies Quarterly* 32 (4). http://dx.doi.org.holycross.idm.oclc.org/10.18061/dsq.v32i4.1641.

Senier, Siobhan, and Clare Barker. 2013. "Introduction." *Journal of Literary and Cultural Disability Studies* 7 (2): 123–140.

Simonsen, Jane E. 2006. *Making Home Work: Domesticity and Native American Assimilation in the American West, 1860–1919*. Chapel Hill: University of North Carolina Press.

Simpson, Audra. 2014. *Mohawk Interruptus: Political Life across the Borders of Settler States*. Durham, NC: Duke University Press.

Spack, Ruth. 2002. *America's Second Tongue: American Indian Education and the Ownership of English, 1860–1900*. Lincoln: University of Nebraska Press.

Standing Bear, Luther. 2006a. *Land of the Spotted Eagle*. Lincoln: University of Nebraska Press.

Standing Bear, Luther. 2006b. *My People the Sioux*. Lincoln: University of Nebraska Press.

Stowe, Harriet Beecher. 1877. "The Indians at St. Augustine." *Christian Union*, April 25.

Street, Bryan. 1995. *Social Literacies: Critical Approaches to Literacy in Development, Ethnography, and Education*. New York: Longman.

Stuart, Harriet Mary. 1915. "Making Our Homes Attractive." *Nez Perce Indian* 1 (21), April 1, 1–3.

Taylor, Diana. 2003. *The Archive and the Repertoire: Performing Cultural Memory in the Americas.* Durham, NC: Duke University Press.

Teuton, Christopher. 2010. *Deep Waters: The Textual Continuum in American Indian Literature.* Lincoln: University of Nebraska Press.

Tomiak, Julie. 2016. "Unsettling Ottawa: Settler Colonialism, Indigenous Resistance, and the Politics of Scale." *Canadian Journal of Urban Research* 25 (1): 1–40.

Townsend, Samuel. 1881a. *School News* 1 (1). Carlisle Indian School, Carlisle, PA. April, 2.

Townsend, Samuel. 1881b. *School News* 1 (10). Carlisle Indian School, Carlisle, PA. March.

Tuck, Eve, and Wayne Yang. 2012. "Decolonization Is Not a Metaphor." *Decolonization: Indigeneity, Education, and Society* 1 (1): 1–40.

Turner, Frederick Jackson. 1921. "The Significance of the Frontier in American History." In *The Frontier in American History*, edited by Frederick Jackson Turner, 1–38. New York: Henry Holt and Company.

Unknown [Samuel Townsend?]. 1880. Editorial published in *School News* 1 (5). 1880. Carlisle Indian School, Carlisle, PA. October, 2.

Utley, Robert M. 1964. "Introduction." In *Battlefield and Classroom: Four Decades with the American Indian, 1867–1904*, by Richard Henry Pratt, xvii–xxvii. New Haven, CT: Yale University Press.

Utley, Robert M. 1974. "The Ordeal of Plenty Horses." *American Heritage* 26 (1). https://www.americanheritage.com/ordeal-plenty-horses.

Vizenor, Gerald. 1994. *Manifest Manners: Narratives on Postindian Survivance.* Lincoln: University of Nebraska Press.

Warrior, Robert. 2005. *The People and the Word: Reading Native Nonfiction.* Minneapolis: University of Minnesota Press.

Washburn, Kathleen. 2012. "New Indians and Indigenous Archives." *Publications of the Modern Language Association* 127 (2): 380–384.

Wexler, Laura. 1994. "Tender Violence: Literary Eavesdropping, Domestic Fiction, and Educational Reform." In *The Culture of Sentiment: Race, Gender, and Sentimentality in the 19th Century*, edited by Shirley Samuels, 9–38. New York: Oxford University Press.

White, Richard. 1991. *The Middle Ground.* Cambridge: Cambridge University Press.

White Bear, Stephen K. 1882. "Speak Only English." *School News* 2 (8). Carlisle Indian School, Carlisle, PA. January, 4.

Wisecup, Kelly. 2013. *Medical Encounters: Knowledge and Identity in Early American Literatures.* Amherst: University of Massachusetts Press.

Wolfe, Patrick. 2006. "Settler Colonialism and the Elimination of the Native." *Journal of Genocide Research* 8 (4): 387–409.

Wyss, Hilary. 2000. *Writing Indians: Literacy, Christianity, and Native Community in Early America.* Amherst: University of Massachusetts Press.

Wyss, Hilary. 2012. *English Letters and Indian Literacies: Reading, Writing, and New England Missionary Schools, 1750–1830.* Philadelphia: University of Pennsylvania Press.

Yandell, Kay. 2012. "The Moccasin Telegraph: Sign-Talk Autobiography and Pretty-Shield, Medicine Woman of the Crows." *American Literature* 84 (3): 533–561.

Zink, Amanda J. 2015. "Carlisle's Writing Circle: Boarding School Texts and the Decolonization of Domesticity." *Studies in American Indian Literatures* 27 (4): 37–65.

Zitkála-Šá. 2003a. *American Indian Stories, Legends, and Other Writings*, edited by Cathy Davidson and Ada Norris. New York: Penguin.

Zitkála-Šá. 2003b. "The School Days of an Indian Girl." In *American Indian Stories, Legends, and Other Writings*, edited by Cathy Davidson and Ada Norris, 87–103. New York: Penguin.

Zitkála-Šá. 2003c. "The Soft Hearted Sioux." In *American Indian Stories, Legends, and Other Writings*, edited by Cathy Davidson and Ada Norris, 118–126. New York: Penguin.

ABOUT THE AUTHOR

Sarah Klotz is assistant professor of English at the College of the Holy Cross. Her research explores the role of literacy in American nation building, using rhetorical theory as a lens to understand race and racialization in the United States. She received the Emergent Researcher Award from the Conference on College Composition and Communication in 2016.

INDEX

Page numbers in italics indicate illustrations.